Brigham Young and the priesthood ban
The lineage criterion

About the author

Matthieu Crouet served as a missionary for the Church of Jesus Christ of Latter-day Saints in the Madagascar Antananarivo Mission from 2000 through 2002.

To help a family in his ward, the mother of which had African ancestors, he agreed to make a comparison between the statements of Church leaders and the accusations of racism made against them. The result was a first essay entitled *Interconfessional Comparison of Perceptions of the Black Skin*: *Jews, Muslims and Christians* with a specific emphasis among Christians on the perception of black skin by the Church of Jesus Christ of Latter-day Saints. This study has not been published.

A short passage of the essay dealt with the priesthood ban. Soon, the author noted the controversy created by the ban and decided to further investigate the topic. This led to a second essay published here.

BRIGHAM YOUNG AND THE PRIESTHOOD BAN

THE LINEAGE CRITERION

Matthieu Crouet

Acknowledgments

I first wish to acknowledge my wife's support. Also Marcel Kahne, without whom this essay would certainly not have been so complete. Our impassioned and often open exchanges constantly drove me to do more research, to better justify and structure my writings. I also wish to thank Thierry Crucy, the translator, and my first readers for their edifying comments which have inspired me to write some passages.

Copyright

ISBN : 978-2-9555053-3-5
Dépôt légal : July 2017
© Matthieu Crouet, 2017
10, rue de l'Etang de la Loy
77400 Saint-Thibault-des-Vignes

Original title : Brigham Young et l'interdiction de prêtrise
Translate by Thierry Crucy

To all priesthood bearers

TABLE OF CONTENTS

David Ransom: *So in retrospect was the Church wrong in that [the ban]?*
President Hinckley: *No I don't think it was wrong. It things, various things happened in different periods. There's a reason for them.*
David Ransom: *What was the reason for that?*
Président Hinckley: *I don't know what the reason was. But I know that we've rectified whatever may have appeared to be wrong at that time.*

(Compass Sundays Nights on ABCTV - *Interview with President Gordon B. Hinckley*, Nov 09, 1997)

One of the most striking changes of the 20th century in the Church of Jesus Christ of Latter-day Saints took place in 1978 when Spencer W. Kimball received a revelation that the priesthood could be conferred on all worthy male members of the Church 12-years old and older with the power to exercise its divine authority[1].

Until then, there had been a ban to withhold the priesthood, which applied to certain men, **erroneously called priesthood ban for black people**. Of course, such terms can only create confusion as they refer to skin color, to racial discrimination which, if it were the case, would originate out of and find their bases in the racist pseudo-theories by the thinkers and scholars of the 17th and 18th centuries for the purpose of supporting the profitable practice of slavery. It would then have been a mistake created and perpetuated by our modern-day prophets influenced by the beliefs of their day. True, it is human to err, but can we really believe that God would have allowed such a mistake?

Today, the Church's official position, clarified in the article entitled *Race and the Priesthood*[2], does not admit that there was an error. After reading it, one can conclude that no explanation given in the past is acknowledged as an official rationale and that one must be careful when dealing with this topic because these ideas echo the then widespread concept of racial inferiority.

Was it a mistake or was there a legitimate reason? Leaders warn against debating about what one does not know[3]. However, **those who say it was a mistake get large media coverage with well-rehearsed rhetoric: the ban was about skin color – With no scriptural support for this – It is a mistake**. The advocates of the legitimate reason, on the other hand, are not very vocal anymore, as they prefer heeding the warnings. There is such confusion between of the conceptual meaning of the terms Cham's curse, lineage, black, slavery, inferiority and priesthood that nobody dares speculate on a legitimate reason.

The rhetoric of those who claim it was a mistake, however, does not hold. The way the ban was applied shows already that this was not the case. **If skin color had been the matter, then no black man could have held the priesthood prior to 1978. Black Africans were affected by the ban, but it did not apply to New Caledonia**

Melanesians, India Dravidians or Australia Aborigines. So skin color could not have been the cause for the ban.

When Church leaders express their personal opinions, they do not admit that a mistake was made, as was exemplified by President Hinckley (1910-2008) during his interview in the Compass Sunday Nights program in 1997: « ***No, I don't think it was wrong*** », or by Dallin H. Oaks who made this comment about the ban in 1988: « *It's not the pattern of the Lord to give reasons. We can put reasons **to commandments** [...]*[4] ».

Brigham Young (1801-1877) justified the ban with these words: « *Any man having one drop of the seed of Cane in him cannot hold the priesthood and if no other prophet spake it before, I will say it now in the name of Jesus Christ. I know it is true and they know it*[5] ».

For Brigham Young, the cause for the ban was lineage. This is supported by Scriptures: Abraham claimed the priesthood because of his lineage (Abraham 1: 5-7), and that Pharaoh had no rights to it because of his lineage (Abraham 1: 27). Nehemiah denied the Levites who could not prove their lineage the right to officiate (Nehemiah 7: 64). In our time, Joseph Smith received a revelation saying that the priesthood was obtained through lineage (D&C 113: 7-8). Jesus Christ declared that he was accomplishing his earthly ministry among people of a certain lineage (Matthew 15: 24). Finally, beside blood lineage, one can become heir to the blessings of Abraham by being adopted into his lineage! (Galatians 3: 27-29 and Abraham 2: 10). Why did Paul need to teach adoption if not to bear witness of the importance of lineage?

This essay does not purport to answer all questions or to provide a set of undeniable arguments. Because of the lack of adequate documents and time, there still remain many gray areas, many speculations, and many points to investigate with the hope that others will do it.

There is, however enough matter to present. It will be divided into seven chapters.

In order to further examine this hypothesis, one must first unlink the topic from the unfounded confused entanglement that links the ban on the priesthood to the pseudo-racist theories of the 17th and 18th centuries. This will be the subject of the first chapter.

In the second chapter, we will introduce the lineage criterion generally. This positive discrimination hurts the feelings of many in today's societies, but it was utilized by Christ during his earthly ministry. We will mainly show how this criterion is still relevant. This chapter will briefly deal with Abraham's favored lineage, and will elaborate on the covenant and promised blessings, including the right to hold the priesthood.

In the third chapter, we will examine the relations maintained by priesthood holders with the other lineages. We will address the crucial issue of mixed marriages and will discuss *the law of the priesthood* which forbids entering into such marriages.

In the fourth chapter, we will discuss Cham's mixed marriage which caused his lineage to be the first one to be denied the priesthood after the Flood. The first but not the last one.

In the fifth chapter, we will study the reaction of Cham's immediate offspring.

In the sixth chapter, we will discuss times when the ban was lifted, first under apostle Peter then under Spencer W. Kimball.

In the last chapter, we will discuss the priesthood from the larger view point of its blessings, particularly of the moment when these blessing are received. We will disprove the theory of the behavior in the preexistence which was put forward to justify the lineage criterion and which has made it difficult to understand the criterion today.

CHAPTER 1

THE BAN ON THE PRIESTHOOD IN THE RACISM IMBROGLIO

In our day, there is an incredible imbroglio which mixes Cham, lineage, black skin, slavery, inferiority and priesthood. Those who say that the ban was a mistake claim that it all came from the racist theories of the 17th and 18th centuries developed to support slavery. If however one examines closely theses notions, one finds that each has its own origin which dates back to way before without any link with any racism. Let us be wary of false accusations.

I
INFERIORITY

According to the dictionary[6], racism is an ideology based on the belief that there is a hierarchy among human groups, which can be accompanied by feelings of hostility and discrimination.

In western societies, the event which gave progressively birth to anti-black racism is to be found in the change in the position of the Catholic Church, which forbad in 1537 that anybody should be reduced to slavery. Until then, the Catholic Church accepted that people be reduced to slavery in order to bring them back to the divine law. The reasoning of the Catholic Church was then as follows: All men are Adam's descendants and, as such, are all equal before God. By rejecting Truth, however, they become slaves to sin, which makes them lose the ability to reason and turns them into brutes. In order to prevent such brutality to spread, it is necessary to curtail the rights of those men, to reduce them to slavery in the vicinity of those who have faith, so that, close to them, they may return to reason. Reports made to the Pope, however showed the contrary: the masters were turning into brutes. In 1537, in at least three letters, one of them, the *Veritas Ipsa* letter dated June 2nd 1537, to all Christians, Paul III (1468-1549) firmly condemned the reduction of any people to slavery, regardless of their faith, under penalty of excommunication: « ***Indians and all other peoples who at a later stage might come to the knowledge of the Christians [...] should not be deprived of their freedom[7]*** ».

The first of the Popes's letters, *Pastorale Officium*, was rescinded in 1538 because it directly challenged Charles the Fifth's authority. In fact, it approved a 1530 imperial decree forbidding the use of Indian slaves, but the Pope did not know that the emperor had rescinded it in 1534. But this was not the end of the matter. In 1542, Charles the Fifth enacted the Leyes Nuevas which forbad the allocation of new encomiendas (where Indians were exploited) and which strictly punished the abuses of those who already owned slaves. These laws led to uprisings and to the death of the viceroy of Peru. Charles the Fifth initiated a process of reflection on how to go about conquering the New World. It led to the Valladolid controversy of 1550 and 1551. Some defended a peaceful and evangelical colonization, others requested the right to resort to slavery to contain the natives' inhuman behaviors. At the end of the debates, both parties proclaimed themselves winners. The Pope did not take a position anymore, but with the mounting criticism, continuing the slavery of the Indians became dangerous. The States distanced themselves from the Catholic Church and from those who questioned the slavery of the Indians.

Racism arose from the reaction of laymen. Since that date, some States, thinkers and scholars, continuously looked for justifications to the practice of cheap human trade in the service of major economic interests. They had to find a way to explain why it was normal to have black slaves, while the slavery of Indians could not be continued. Two major lay arguments were developed beginning in the 17th century, but mostly in the 18th century: because they are an inferior race (polygenism) and because their nature so requires (theory of climates).

1
Polygenism

All men are equal because they all descend from the same man, Adam. Would they still be equal if they did not descend from the same man? **Polygenism states that there are human races or species without common ancestor or family tie**. The first to propose such theory was Frenchman Isaac de Lapeyrère (1596-1676) in his 1655 treaty on preadamites[8]. His thesis found an echo with several scholars, among them Frenchman Voltaire (1694-1778) in his 1734 Treaty of Metaphysics[9], and American Samuel George Morton (1799-1851) who is considered to be at the origin of scientific racism[10].

2
The Theory of Climates

The other theory which found an echo in Western societies is the Theory of Climates, the reintroduction of which is ascribed to Frenchman Charles-Louis de Secondat, baron de La Brède et de Montesquieu (1689-1755), in his book *The spirit of laws*. The theory can be traced back to Hippocrate's book, *Air, water, places* (circa 400 b.c.) and it was used at least since the 11th century in Eastern societies[11]. Even though this theory, at first sight, does not make any reference to skin color, **it shows people in hot climates as aggressive, and having little reason and not much morals**: « *If we draw near the south, we fancy ourselves entirely removed from the verge of morality; here the strongest passions are productive of all manner of crimes, each man endeavouring, let the means be what they will, to indulge his inordinate desires [...]The heat of the climate may be so excessive as to deprive the body of all vigour and strength. Then the faintness is communicated to the mind; there is no curiosity, no enterprise, no generosity of sentiment* » (The spirit of laws XIV, II). Because of their nature, these men would work only under coercion, which would justify slavery: « *There are countries where the excess of heat enervates the body, and renders men so slothful and dispirited that nothing but the fear of chastisement can oblige them to perform any* *laborious duty: slavery is there more reconcilable to reason* » and the author concludes: « ***as all men are born equal, slavery must be accounted unnatural, though in some countries it be founded on natural reason*** » (The spirit of laws XV, VII). This reasoning inspired Germans Johann Friedrich Blumenbach (1752-1840) and Emmanuel Kant (1724-1804), who developed the degenerationist theory, according to which some people degenerated because of the climate, sometimes irreversibly. First meant were the African countries.

In our Western societies, the concept of the inferiority of black people developed from the racist theories of the 17th and 18th centuries. This inferiority was supposed to be the consequence either of existing unequal human races as they are not related with one another, or of a climate which irreversibly dulled the minds of certain peoples. This had nothing to do with the Bible.

II
CHAM'S CURSE

Christianity neither taught the theory of climates nor did it accept polygenism. It has always considered men as being equal, made of one blood[12]. Christianity is mixed with racism by *the Cham's curse* even though its sources are to be found in remote centuries and it never mentions inferiority. Let us see what this « curse » is about and how it differs from racism in the aspects under which it is known today: skin color and slavery.

1
Skin color

Ancient sources trace black skin back to a fault that Cham committed without mentioning that it caused any inferiority.

Among Jews, two stories with different causes were told: The first one is found in the Taanit Treaty in the Jerusalem Talmud (around the 2nd century AD): Ham broke the rule against sexual relationships in the Ark and as a result « *went forth darkened* ». The second one is told in the Bereshit Rabba (written between the 5th and 6th century AD): Ham sees his father's nakedness under the tent and does not turn away his eyes. Noah hears about it and says to Ham: « *Your children shall be born black and ugly* ». For the Jews, however, in the fruit of his seed, only the first born, Kush, and his offspring are affected. No reference is made to any inferiority.

Among Muslims, only the first cause is mentioned: Ibn Hichâm (dead circa 830) tells the great lines of the story of the arch, and attributes them to Wahb ibn Munabbih, a convert to Islam (dead circa 730). In the 10th Century, At-Tabari (839-923) credits a safe Moslem source, Ibn Ishaq (704-767), the Prophet's biographer, a sexual assault by Ham on his wife in the Ark, a prayer on Noah's part requesting that his seed might be adulterated, and that seed might consequently be black. No reference is made to any inferiority.

13

Among Christians, the second cause is mentioned: Cham sees his father's nakedness. When Noah learns about it, he curses him. Ephrem the Syrian (306-373) wrote: « *the face of Canaan and his father Ham became black*[13] ». For Isho' dad of Merv, Syrian Bishop of the Christian church of Haditha (circa 850) [When Noah cursed Canaan], « *Instantly, by the force of the curse, his face and entire body became black. This is the black color which has persisted in his descendants*[14] ». Lastly, for Abū l-Faradj Al 'Ibrī (1225-1286), better known as Bar Hebraeus, a Syrian Christian author of Jewish ascent: « *And Ham, the father of Canaan, saw the nakedness of his father and showed [it] to his two brothers. That is why Canaan was cursed and not Ham, and with the very curse he became black and the blackness was transmitted to his descendants*[15] ». Along with this story, Ephrem the Syria also teaches that Cain became black after murdering Abel: « *Abel was bright as the light, but the murderer (Cain) was dark as the darkness*[16] ». In the Book of Adam, an apocryphal book from the Christian Armenia of the 5th or 6th century, it is also written: « *And the Lord was wroth with Cain. He beat Cain's face with hail, which blackened like coal, and thus he remained with a black face*[17] ». Cham's marriage to one of Cain's descendants, mentioned earlier in this study, made his descendants black skinned through their mother, even though they already were through their father. Once again, no reference is made however to any inferiority.

Thus, the origin of the black skin as the consequence of a fault of the ancestor has no relation to 17th and 18th century racism. Its sources date further back and go against it: no inferiority, no hot climate dulling the minds of people; on the contrary an ancestor common to all men.

2
Slavery

Ancient sources trace slavery back to a fault that Cham committed without mentioning that it caused any inferiority.

There is only one story: Cham sees his father's nakedness and Noah said: « *Cursed be Canaan; a servant of servants shall he be unto his brethren. And he said, blessed be the Lord God of Shem; and Canaan shall be his servant. God shall enlarge Japheth, and he shall dwell in the tents of Shem; and Canaan shall be his servant*[18] ».

The story is strange however. Why was Canaan cursed? There are several acts. Cham and his sons rebelled against Noah's authority. See chapter five. Cham did not see his father's nakedness but his father's priesthood clothing and stole it from him. Canaan had broken his oath and taken possession of lands which had not been allotted to him during the sharing of the land by Noah while he had predicted wars and slavery for whoever would break his oath. **It's the rebel's behavior which leads to war and**

slavery. Slavery is temporal and will be done away at the return to the divine law.

Before 1537, the Catholic Church accepted the slavery of peoples, considered to be of low morality in order to put an end to their abuses (cannibalism, human sacrifices…) until they would come back to the law of God.

Later on, the Dutch Protestants admitted the slavery of the black Africans. Jean Louis Hannemann, in his 1677 essay *Curiosum Scrutinium nigritudinis posterorum Cham i.e. Aethiopum*, mentions the fact that the Ethiopians became slaves because of Cham's curse[19]. The Anglicans followed suite. The Catholic Church remained silent but some of its local leaders subscribed to this justification so much so that during the Vatican I council (1869-1870), a group 65 bishops approached the Pope with a postulatum requesting that the holy father lift the curse upon Cham's sons[20].

Here again, the sources are ancient. The protestants repeated Origen's statement (185-253), in *Homily on Genesis* 16:1 which said about the Egyptians: « *On the contrary, Pharaoh easily reduced the Egyptian people to bondage to himself and it is not written that he resorted to force there, for the Egyptians are prone to a degenerate life and quickly sink to every slavery of the vices. Look at the origin of the race and you will discover that their father Cham, who had laughed at his father's nakedness, deserved a judgment of this kind, that his son Canaan should be a servant to his brothers, in which case the condition of bondage would prove*

16

the wickedness of his conduct. Not without merit, therefore, does the discolored posterity imitate the ignobility of the race[21] *».* **Origen's purpose, however, was to explain why Cham's descendants often found themselves in a condition of slavery because of their morals, not to justify its large scale practice.**

The same claim was made among Muslims. Ibn Khaldun (1332-1406), in his book *Prolégomènes de l'Histoires des Berbères,* declared: « *Some genealogists who had no knowledge of the true nature of beings imagined that the Blacks are the descendants of Ham, the son of Noah, and that they were characterized by black colour as a result of a curse put upon him by his father, which manifested itself in Ham's colour and the slavery that God inflicted upon his descendants* ». Ibn Khaldun, however, challenged this assumption because in the Eastern societies of his time there already existed a non-religious anti-black racism, which he personally embraced. He already invoked the theory of climates to conclude that black Africans « *look rather like wild animals* », and « *they do not deserve to be accounted among men* ».

Therefore, the concept that slavery was a consequence of Cham's curse has no link to the racism of the 17th and 18th centuries. Its sources are older and go against it. It affirms that a morally loose conduct to slavery until the people come back to the divine law, but does not mention a different human species or a hot climate dulling the minds of people without hope

of redemption and whose natural condition is to remain forever in slavery.

III
PRIESTHOOD

Neither aspect of Cham's curse (skin color or slave condition) has to do with the racist theories of the 17th and 18th centuries. How then can one believe that the priesthood ban, a purely religious matter, can be linked to racism?

Brigham Young linked Cham's priesthood ban to his marriage: It was because he married one of Cain's descendants that he cannot pass the priesthood on to his lineage.

This argument of forbidden marriage leading to the prohibition to pass on the priesthood takes up neither the arguments used by laymen to justify the inferiority of black people nor those used by religious people to justify skin color and slavery. If Brigham Young had meant to link priesthood to skin color, he would have presented the ban as a consequence of what Cham did under the tent.

The justification given by Brigham Young is also supported by ancient sources. It is the subject of the next chapters. The Levi aramaic document (3rd century B.C.) found among the Dead Sea scrolls already taught prohibition to marry for reason of lineage as priesthood law. Similarly, Rachi (1040-

1105) mentioned that Abba Bar Kahana taught in the 4th century that Cain's lineage had survived the Flood.

CHAPTER 2

THE LINEAGE CRITERION

To say that black people were not allowed to hold the priesthood is an unfortunate shortcut which implies that such prohibition had to do with skin color, whereas not all black people were under the ban.

While answers given sometimes refer to black people, other statements by leaders clarify what the ban was about. Bruce R. McConkie (1915-1985), three years after the 1978 revelation confirmed that it was a ban which applied to one lineage: « *The ancient curse is no more. **The seed of Cain and Ham and Canaan and Egyptus and Pharaoh** (Abr. 1: 20-27; Moses 5: 16-41; 7:8, 22) – now have power to rise up and bless Abraham as their father. All these, Gentile in lineage, may now come and inherit by adoption all the blessings of Abraham, Isaac, and Jacob (Rom. 8: 14-24; 9:4; Gal. 4:5; Eph. 1:5; Teachings, pp. 149-50)*[22] ». Moreover, ten years after the revelation, in a talk given on May 1988, during a worldwide broadcast celebrating the 159th anniversary of the restauration of the priesthood, Gordon B. Hinckley, then counselor in the First Presidency, declared that they were commemorating several important events that day, one of them being: « ***The revelation under which the priesthood became available to all worthy men, regardless of lineage***[23] ».

Our perception of lineages is a very poor one. For today's society, lineage does not make much sense any more. We do not hesitate in quoting a few individual scriptures in order to deny this criterion (I). Christ applied it however (II) and it remains valid today (III). This lineage criterion is mostly about a favored lineage, Abraham's, Isaac's and Jacob's. Its particular statute is based on a covenant comprised of commandments and promises. This favoritism however must be mitigated in the lineages descending from Abraham and even more at the individual level (IV).

I
INDIVIDUAL SCRIPTURES

With our individualistic vision, we interpret too rapidly certain Scriptures about the individual nature of sin (1) and vain genealogies (2).

1
The individual nature of sin

Edward L. Kimball, in the footnote on page 10 of his essay *Spencer W. Kimball and the Revelation on Priesthood*, wonders about the apparent contradiction between several scriptures: « *The Article of Faith stating that "men will be punished for their own sins and not for Adam's transgression[24]" emphasized individual responsibility, and Ezekiel 18:20 is critical of guilt by lineage [The soul that sinneth, il shall die. The son shall not bear the iniquity of the father, neither the father bear the iniquity of the son: the righteousness of the righteous shall be upon him, and the wickedness of the wicked shall be upon him[25]].See also 2 Nephi 26:33 (black and white are all alike unto God); Moroni 8:12 (little children who die without baptism are alive in Christ). Still, the idea of a blessed or cursed lineage is not foreign to the scriptures. Notable examples are the descendants of Abraham, a blessed lineage (Gen. 22:17–18), and the Lamanites in the Book of Mormon, a cursed lineage (2 Ne. 5:21)[26] ».*

There is no contradiction there. One word appears in both passages, *sin* with carries, for the sinner who does not repent, the consequence that he cannot return and live in God's presence. This introspection is personal and whether **the doors to the celestial kingdom open deepens solely on our own sins**, not on those of someone else, ancestor or not.

But the actions of the ancestors, good or bad, affect their descendants. Adam's transgression, mentioned in the second article of faith, undeniably affected the live of his posterity: The first consequence was the very existence of the posterity. Had there not been a transgression, man would not be. Adam would have remained alone with Eve, not being subject to death, in the presence of our Father in heavens, without any possibility for evolution. By partaking of the forbidden fruit, they were blessed with a posterity, with a knowledge of good and evil, with the joy of redemption and with the possibility for eternal growth. They became, however, also subject, as all of their descendants, to disease, and physical death, experiencing hard work, pain and sorrow.

The influence of ascendance on life conditions is particularly clearly set out in the Book of Mormon. Many passages refer to the ***traditions of the fathers*** which misled the Lamanite posterity by passing on false beliefs and bad behaviors, which deprived them of blessings[27]. For example, the book of Alma mentions: « *Thus they were a very indolent people, many of whom did worship idols, and the curse of God had fallen upon them because of the traditions of their fathers[28]* ». The posterity misses the Gospel and the spiritual blessings which it brings, mainly because of traditions of the fathers which mislead it. The daily condition of the descendants is undeniably impacted by the actions of the ancestors.

Even though our mortal condition is affected by our ancestors' behavior, only our works and sins will be taken into consideration to determine our right to return and live in God's presence.

2
Vain genealogies

There is another apparent contradiction in scriptural passages regarding genealogies as vain. Paul teaches Timothy: « *Neither give heed to endless genealogies, which minister questions, rather than godly edifying which is in faith[29]* ». He gives the same piece of advice to Titus: « *avoid foolish questions, and genealogies, and contentions, and strivings about the law; for they are unprofitable and vain[30]* ».

There again, there is no real contradiction. In fact, in the time of Christ, the Jews believed that they were the only ones would could obtain salvation as the chosen people[31]. One proved his membership within the chosen people through one's genealogy, which, consequently the Jews kept very preciously. **The ancestry was examined even more closely when a man claimed the right to exercise the priesthood as one of Aaron's descendants. If he could not prove his lineage, he was deprived of the priesthood**[32]. Herod was Idumean. He was envious of the noble origin of the Jews. He ordered the destruction of the public records, including of the genealogical tables. Then the Jews could refer to their origins only from memory, and tried to reconstitute endless and uncertain genealogies[33].

This Jewish dispute is a clear proof of the importance of the lineage to obtain the priesthood. As we will see soon, these relentless efforts to reconstitute genealogies were, however of much less interest in Paul's day. He taught Timothy and Titus not to waste time in vain genealogies, because the right to become members and to hold the priesthood had just been extended to the heathens through a new way of entering Abraham's lineage: adoption.

II
APPLICATION OF THE CRITERION BY CHRIST

When Christ sent his apostles out to preach the Gospel, he commanded them specifically: « *Go not into the way of the Gentiles, and into any city of the Samaritans enter ye not: But go rather to the lost sheep of the house of Israel[34]* ».

He himself had received this recommendation from God: « ***I am not sent but unto the lost sheep of the house of Israel[35]*** ». The authors of the Gospels confirm that the Lord exercised his ministry among the people of Israel. Thus, this people had two favors from God: They were the first to know the Gospel and the Lord was among them during his earthly ministry.

Two favors from God of which the Jews did not take advantage because they did not recognize their Savior. So, Paul and Barnabas told the Jews, after baptism was made available to the Gentiles: « *It was necessary that the word of God should first have been spoken to you: but seeing ye put it from you, and judge yourselves unworthy of everlasting life, lo, we turn to the Gentiles[36]* ».

III
APPLYING THE CRITERION TO OUR TIME

Sometime between Christ's earthly ministry and Paul's epistles, Peter received a revelation informing him that the house of Israel was not the only one which should receive the Gospel and that heathens could also be baptized[37]. This reversal legitimately raises the question of lineage. Had lineage, so important before, now disappeared?

On the contrary, Paul's answer confirms that the lineage criterion still applies. The Gospel is the privilege of Abraham's lineage. And it is available to the heathens because baptism incorporates them into Abraham's posterity through adoption : « *For as many of you as have been baptized into Christ have put on Christ [...] And if ye be Christ's, then are ye Abraham's seed, and heirs according to the promise*[38] ».

This promise was made to Abraham: « *For as many as receive this Gospel shall be called after thy name, and shall be accounted thy seed, and shall rise up and bless thee, as their father*[39] ».

Joseph Fielding Smith (1876-1972) further indicates that this connection to Abraham through adoption takes place more specifically through Jacob's lineage: « *Every person who embraces the gospel becomes of the house of Israel. In other words, they become members of the chosen lineage, or Abraham's children through Isaac and Jacob unto whom the promise was made* ». He adds a little later: « *Those who are not literal descendants of Abraham and Israel must become such, and when they are baptized and confirmed they are grafted into the tree and are entitled to all the rights and privileges as heirs*[40] ».

John A. Widtsoe (1872-1952) goes even further by affirming that a descendant by blood will lose his lineage if he rejects the Gospel: « *All who accept God's plan for his children on earth and who live it are the children of Abraham. Those who reject the gospel, whether children in the flesh, or others, forfeit the promises made to Abraham and are not children of Abraham*[41]».

Nephi prophesied that this would happen in the future: « *And because of the words which have been spoken ye need not suppose that the Gentiles are utterly destroyed. For behold, I say unto you that as many of the Gentiles as will repent are the covenant people of the Lord; and as many of the Jews as will not repent shall be cast off*[42] ».

In our day, it is still entirely justified when a patriarch states in patriarchal blessings the connection to Jacob through one of the twelve tribes.

Modern revelation also confirms that the priesthood today is held by virtue of lineage. We read in Doctrine and Covenants: « Questions by Elias Higbee: *What is meant by the command in Isaiah, 52d chapter, 1st verse, which saith: Put on thy strength, O Zion - and what people had Isaiah reference to?* **He had reference to those whom God should call in the last days, who should hold the power of priesthood** *to bring again Zion, and the redemption of Israel;* **and to put on her strength is to put on the authority of the priesthood, which she, Zion, has a right to by lineage;** *also to return to that power which she had lost*[43] *»*.

So, today men hold this priesthood only as Abraham's descendants belonging to his lineage by blood or by adoption.

IV
ABRAHAM'S FAVORED LINEAGE

The Scriptures are replete with lineage blessings. For example, we have, more or less developed, each of the blessings of Jacob's twelve sons[44], repeated by Moses several centuries later in order to remind each lineage of their particular blessings[45]. We also find the blessings given to the descendants of Ishmael and Isaac[46], Ephraim and Manasseh[47], and Laman and Lemuel[48]. Pharao's lineage was specifically blessed with wisdom[49], which may explain the unparalleled longevity of the Egyptian civilizations, which spanned three thousand years.

But no lineage received such promises as Abraham's. They were given in return for the people's commitment to have only one God and to worship according to his commandments. All of

30

this was developed and commented as the **Abrahamic covenant.** There are four promises: promise to be the covenant people (1), promise of a land (2), promise of a posterity (3), and promise to benefit from the priesthood (4). Some of these promises are to be kept during this life, some only during the next one, within the people of the covenant.

1
Being the people of the covenant

Whereas his father, Terach, had turned away from God's way, Abram sought after the blessings of his ancestors. He knew that he belonged to a lineage which was entitled to know the Gospel and hold the priesthood. He found favor in the sight of the Lord, who established his covenant with him and with his posterity as follows: « *I will establish my covenant between me and thee and thy seed after thee in their generations for an everlasting covenant, **to be a God unto thee, and to thy seed after thee***[50] ». As a sign of the covenant, the Lord changed Abram's name to Abraham and Sarai's name to Sarah[51] and required that every male be circumcised at the age of eight days[52].

For God, the covenant thus entered into with Abraham's lineage is not a simple contract that each of the parties can breach at any time. True, God is bound only as long as the people walks with him in all integrity[53], but beside the reciprocal commitments, this covenant is about love,

31

compassion, forgiveness and patience as is evidenced in the following Scriptures: « *Behold, I have graven thee upon the palms of my hands*[54] », « *Can a woman forget her sucking child, that she should not have compassion on the son of her womb? yea, they may forget, yet will I not forget thee?*[55] », « *How often would I have gathered thy children together, even as a hen gathereth her chickens under her wings, and ye would not!*[56] » and after and beyond the foretold apostasy: « *Then will I remember my covenant with Jacob, and also my covenant with Isaac, and also my covenant with Abraham will I remember; and I will remember the land. The land also shall be left of them, and shall enjoy her sabbaths, while she lieth desolate without them: and they shall accept of the punishment of their iniquity: because, even because they despised my judgments, and because their soul abhorred my statutes. And yet for all that, when they be in the land of their enemies, I will not cast them away, neither will I abhor them, to destroy them utterly, and to break my covenant with them: for I am the Lord their God. But I will for their sakes remember the covenant of their ancestors, whom I brought forth out of the land of Egypt in the sight of the heathen, that I might be their God: I am the Lord*[57] ».

Whole generations of the chosen people however were born during the apostasy and could not receive the promised blessings. Only in the next life will they be able to receive them.

2
A land

The second promise made to Abraham and his posterity is a land as an inheritance. Genesis recalls the Lord's words to Abraham: « *And I will give unto thee, and to thy seed after thee, the land wherein thou art a stranger, all the land of Canaan, for an everlasting possession*[58] ». The book of Abraham mentions this same promise in similar terms: « *Arise, [...] for I have purposed to take thee away out of Haran and to make of thee a minister to bear my name in a strange land which I will give unto thy seed after thee for an everlasting possession, when they hearken to my voice*[59] ».

Abraham, however, did not receive this blessing. He never possessed the land of Canaan. Over the approximately 3900 years which have passed since the promise was made, many of his descendants could not possess it either. Many generations born during the diaspora could not receive it either.

3
A posterity

The third promise made to Abraham affecting also his descendants is a posterity without end. The Lord told Abraham: « *I will multiply thee exceedingly [...] thou shalt be a father of many nations*[60] ».

Abraham obtained this posterity without end, but certain of his descendants did not. Some died too young or were not able to get married, others were sterile and some posterities died out.

4
The priesthood

The fourth promise made to Abraham is that of holding the priesthood. A promise, according to the Book of Abraham, that Abraham was seeking not because of a personal revelation in which God would have promised it to him, but which he claimed because of his lineage : « *I sought for the blessings of the fathers, and the right whereunto I should be ordained to administer the same [...] I became a rightful heir, a High Priest, holding the right belonging to the fathers [...]I sought for mine appointment unto the Priesthood according to the appointment of God unto the fathers concerning the seed*[61] ».

After explaining his own situation, it is not without reason that he mentions his rival, Pharao's situation. The latter also claims the right to the priesthood through lineage, a lineage which Abraham says is banned from the priesthood: « **Now, Pharaoh being of that lineage by which he could not have the right of Priesthood**, *notwithstanding the Pharaohs would fain claim it from Noah, through Ham*[62] ». **The Scripture does not say that this lineage did not have the priesthood, but that it had no right to the**

priesthood. At this point in our study, we will not mention the reasons why Pharaoh's lineage was banned from holding the priesthood, but the scriptures are clear: **holding the priesthood for Abraham and the priesthood ban for Pharaoh are both justified by their respective lineages.**

This being said, not all of Abraham's descendants could hold it or even receive its blessings.

Some might think it unjust that God favored Abraham's posterity in general and the people of Israel in particular. As a start, we can qualify these favors given their limited application on the earth. Furthermore, on the earth, God's justice does not lie in a strict equality between men or lineages, but it gives us the opportunity to receive the same blessings in the life to come. It only depends on our obedience while on earth to laws which our conscience tells us are just.

The same blessings are available to all those who will be found worthy, through temple ordinances on behalf of the dead. Every time we accomplish ordinances for deceased persons, they receive baptism by proxy, become members of Abraham's posterity and hear pronounced upon their heads the four promises made to Abraham: to belong to the covenant people, to obtain a land, to have a posterity and to hold the priesthood.

How about preserving the chosen lineage? Did that lineage have the right to mix with other lineages? If so, did the marriage allow to pass the priesthood on to the posterity?

CHAPTER 3

GENEALOGICAL PURITY,
A PRIESTHOOD LAW

Within the people of Israel, priesthood holders have always been a special group subject to stricter rules regarding the aspects of daily life, marriage being one of them.

Genealogical purity is a priesthood law (I). A lack of it prevents passing the priesthood to the descendants from the unlawful marriage (II).

I
GENEALOGICAL PURITY

Among the Dead Sea scrolls were some of the oldest Jewish records found to this day: the Aramaic Levi document from the 3rd century B.C. and the Book of Tobit from the 2nd century B.C. These records deal precisely with our subject (1). They shed a new light on some Bible passages (2). Today, even non-LDS scholars mention genealogical purity (3).

1
The Aramaic Levi Document[63]
And The Book of Tobit[64]

The Aramaic Levi Document describes Levi's ordination to the priesthood by his father, Jacob; then a visit to the family by grand-father, Isaac, who teaches him the laws of the priesthood.

The Aramaic Levi Document mentions the meeting as follows: « *And Isaac our father saw all of us and blessed us and rejoiced. When he learned that I was a priest of the Most High God, the Lord of heaven, he began to instruct me and to teach me the law of the priesthood and he said to me: « Levi, my son, beware of all uncleanliness and all sin, your judgment is greater than that of all flesh. Now my son I will show you the true law and I will not hide any word from you to teach you* **the law of the priesthood**. *First of all, beware my son of all fornication, impurity and of all harlotry. And* **do take a wife from my family** *and do not defile your seed with harlots* **since you are holy seed**, *and sanctify your seed like the holy place since you are called a holy priest for all the seed of Abraham. You are near to God and near to all his holy ones. Now, be pure in your flesh from every impurity of mankind*[65]*»* ».

The Book of Tobit relates similar words from Tobit to his son, Tobias: « *Beware, my son, of every kind of fornication. First of all,* **marry a woman from among the descendants of your ancestors; do not marry a foreign woman, who is not of your father's tribe; for we are the descendants of the prophets. Remember, my son, that Noah, Abraham, Isaac, and Jacob, our ancestors of old, all took wives from among their kindred;** *they were blessed in their children, and their posterity will inherit the land*[66] ».

The first comment at this point: the rule was not only to avoid committing idolatry with foreign women, but really to choose a wife among one's clan, one's family.

This rule echoes several Old Testament passages.

2
Bible passages

Abraham applied the rule to his son, Isaac, heir of the covenant[67], by commanding his servant to look for a wife from his homeland for his son: « *Abraham said to his eldest servant of his house [...]: Put, I pray thee, thy hand under my thigh: And I will make thee swear by the Lord, the God of heaven, and the God of the earth, that thou shalt not take a wife unto my son of the daughters of the Canaanites, among whom I dwell : **But thou shalt go unto my country, and to my kindred, and take a wife unto my son Isaac**[68]* ».

Isaac later gave his son, Jacob, the same commandment: « *And Isaac called Jacob, and blessed him, and charged him, and said unto him, Thou shalt not take a wife of the daughters of Canaan. **Arise, go to Padanaram, to the house of Bethuel thy mother's father; and take thee a wife from thence of the daughters of Laban thy mother's brother**[69]* ».

On the opposite, Rebecca reacts very vividly when her son Esaü decides to marry some of Heth's daughters: « *I am weary of my life because of the daughters of Heth: if Jacob take a wife of the daughters of Heth, such as these which are of the daughters of the land, what good shall my life do me?[70] ».*

The reference to « *the family* » rules out any marriage with remote lineages. Without having to define what is or is not of the family, **if Cham married one of Cain's descendants, he indisputably broke this priesthood law** since Cain's lineage is the most remote of all. Cham would have had to go back to the first man, Adam, in order to find the ancestor he had in common with his wife.

3
Scholars' comments

In her book *Gentile Impurities and Jewish Identities: Intermarriage and Conversion from the Bible to the Talmud[71]* Christine Hayes makes a major contribution by recognizing **genealogical impurities**, beside ritual impurities and moral impurities. Based on the concept of « *holy race* » dear to Ezra[72], genealogical impurity is established as soon as the priest lineage mixes with foreign women.

The prohibition is not limited to foreign women. The « *holy race* » cannot mix within « *the family* » with « *harlots[73]* ». As John Kampen states, the Biblical definition of harlot is different from today's; it allows all forbidden sexual practices[74], including forbidden marriages.

Flavius Josephus wrote: « *For our forefathers [...] made provision that the stock of the priests should continue unmixed, and pure*[75] ».

The right to officiate in rites of the priesthood was verified by examining the genealogical records and witnesses[76]. In case of doubt, the applicant's request was denied[77].

In order to avoid questionable lineages within the family itself, Rachi (1040-1105) taught in the Guerama Yevamot (84b): « *A Cohen, if he can marry a Cohen's daughter, should not marry an Israel. Which means that a Cohen who has the opportunity to marry a Cohen's daughter who suits him, must marry her and must not take as a wife an Israel woman* ».

Christine Hayes further contributes to the study by adding that, contrary to the other impurities, the genealogical impurity prevents one from transmitting the priesthood to his descendants (II).

II
IMPOSSIBLE TRANSMISSION
TO THE DESCENDANTS

Christine Hayes distinguishes between three types of impurities: ritual, moral and genealogical.

Ritual impurities are unavoidable personal impurities related to daily life: birth, death, menstruations, disease… These impurities result in a reduced communication of the person with Deity. They can be remedied through purification rituals.

Moral impurities are personal impurities caused by immoral acts like sexual depravity or idolatry. One can be purified from them through punishment and repentance.

Genealogical impurities are inherited. They are due to the presence among the ascendants of one or more ancestors forbidden by divine law, which defile the lineage. Such impurities cannot be remedied by rituals or by repentance. They deprive those who carry them of the priesthood. Therefore, the only way not to contract these impurities is not to contract a forbidden marriage. If this is already done, the wives and the offspring born of these unions must be sent back so as not to be defile the rest of the lineage.

A perfect example of this rule is to be found at the time of Ezra and Nehemiah. When Cyrus' edict in 538 B.C. allowed the Israelites to return to Judea, a small number of them decided to return to Palestine. 114, among them 17 priests, 6 Levites, and 4 temple officers married daughters from the peoples of the land, comprised among others of Canaanites, Edomites, Egyptians, Moabites, Ammonites. The first three are Cham's descendants, the last two of which refused to help the Israelites. Ezra had the men take an oath to send back the wives and the children born of them and observed that they respected it only partially[78]. Later, Nehemiah was more successful. A priest in these circumstances could not pass the priesthood on to his posterity.

So, marriage in and of itself can result in the loss of the priesthood to the posterity, even when the wife and children would have embraced the beliefs of the husband or father. Besides, for the Israelites, such marriage was not recognized. It was deemed null and void. Those guilty of contracting it did not need to get a divorce, since a divorce could take place only after a marriage was considered valid.

Now, did Cham also lose this right to the priesthood for his descendants by marrying outside the family?

CHAPTER 4

CHAM'S FORBIDDEN MARRIAGE

The reason why Cham's lineage was denied the right to hold the priesthood is known since the priesthood-ban restoration. We find it mentioned as soon as 1849[79] : Cham married outside his family when he espoused one of Cain's descendants (1), a lineage which had soon lost its right to hold the priesthood (2).

I
CHAM'S MARRIAGE
TO ONE OF CAIN'S DESCENDANTS

Was one of Cain's descendants in Noah's ark? After he murdered Abel, Cain left with several children and grand-children to another area farther east. The Book of Moses makes it clear that Cain's posterity had no place with the rest of Adam's posterity[80]. As time passed, however, Adam's people also became wicked and wound up establishing exchanges with Cain's posterity. Did one of his descendants become the wife of one of the passengers of the Ark? The idea that Cain's lineage survived the Flood is very old (1). The woman would be Naama (2) Cham's wife (3). We will examine what the Book of Abraham says about it (4).

1
The survival of Cain's lineage after the Flood

The idea that Cain's lineage survived the Flood is very old. Rabbi Abba Bar Kahana stated it in the **4th century B.C.**, according to Rachi, who mentioned it in a commentary on *Genesis Rabbah*[81].

2
Naama, the wife

Genesis lists part of Cain's descendants. Naama, Lamech's daughter and Tubal-Cain's sister is the last of the line. And, under the passage of Genesis Rabbah « *and Tubal-cain's sister was Na'amah* », Rachi noted: « *R. Abba b. Kahana said: « Na'amah was the wife of Noah* ».

The Bible does not say as much. It only mentions: « *The sister of Tubalcain was Naamah*[82] ». **Let us point out, however, that Biblical texts usually do not mention the names of female children, except if they play a part in future events. Based on this and on the fact that her name is given at this point in the story, one does not see the point in mentioning her unless she is the wife of one of the people who entered the Ark.**

Contrary to Abba Bar Kahana's words quoted by Rachi, the Book of the Just, or Book of Jasher, also mentions a Naama, Noah's wife but Enoch's daughter of Seth's lineage : « *Noah went and took a wife, and he chose Naamah the daughter of Enoch*[83] » (a marriage within the family). Now the origins of this book, quoted twice in the Bible[84], are supposed to be older, and to date back to the 9th or 10th century B.C. The Book of Tobit previously mentioned also states that Noah married *within the family*[85]. **If Noah's Naama belonged to Seth's lineage, then whom did Naama, from Cain's lineage, mentioned in the scriptures marry? It can only be one of Noah's sons whom we still have to identify.**

3
Cham, the husband

Richard Cumberland (1631-1718) was the one to suggest that the Naama of Cain's lineage was Cham's wife based on Plutarch's works (46-125). Plutarch, a Greek who lived in ancient Rome, affirmed that Cronos was Cham **after comparing the Greek gods to biblical characters**. Richard Cumberland concurred with the comparison and noted that the first name of Cronos' wife, sometimes called Nemanus, according to Plutarch, was the Greek form for the Hebrew Naama and, consequently, it is indeed Cham who must have been married to the Naama of Cain's lineage[86].

The origins of mythologies are supposedly based on fact, on memories of the lives of ancestors, greatly distorted over time. Plutarch is not the only one who attempted to make these comparisons. Many others did also and their similarities point to the same conclusions. For instance, some say that Erakles is Nimrod, which would confirm the lineage, Cham as Cronos: Erakles (Nimrod), son of Zeus (Cush), son of Cronos (Cham), son of Ouranos, the first god (Noah).

According to the oldest references, Cain's lineage would have survived through a woman who was not Noah's wife. A study of mythology makes one lean towards the suggestion that it was Cham's wife.

4
Contribution of the Book of Abraham

A passage of scripture deals with Pharaoh's lineage, clarifying that it is banned from the priesthood. One can learn much from it because it is very precise: « ***Now this king of Egypt was a descendant from the loins of Ham***, *and was a partaker of the blood of the Canaanites by birth. From this descent sprang all the Egyptians, and thus the blood of the Canaanites was preserved in the land. The land of Egypt being first discovered by a woman, who was the daughter of Ham, and the daughter of Egyptus, which in the Chaldean signifies Egypt, which signifies that which is forbidden; When this woman discovered the land it was under water, who afterward settled her sons in it; and thus,* ***from***

49

Ham, sprang that race which preserved the curse in the land. Now the first government of Egypt was established by Pharaoh, the eldest son of Egyptus, the daughter of Ham, and it was after the manner of the government of Ham, which was patriarchal. Pharaoh, being a righteous man, established his kingdom and judged his people wisely and justly all his days, seeking earnestly to imitate that order established by the fathers in the first generations, in the days of the first patriarchal reign, even in the reign of Adam, and also of **Noah, his father, who** *blessed him with the blessings of the earth, and with the blessings of wisdom, but* **cursed him as pertaining to the Priesthood.** *Now,* **Pharaoh being of that lineage by which he could not have the right of Priesthood, notwithstanding the Pharaohs would fain claim it from Noah, through Ham**[87] ».

The main line of the passage, bolded in the text, is highlighted by a **syllogism**:

> 1/ Pharaoh descends from Cham
> 2/ Cham was cursed by his father Noah regarding the priesthood
> 3/ so Pharaoh belongs to this lineage banned from the priesthood.

Abraham uses a figure of speech to stress the fact that the ban came through Cham and that affects the latter's lineage.

Hugh Nibley (1910-2005) states that Pharaoh was denied the priesthood because his lineage was matriarchal, not because of Cham[88]. That the priesthood would have been obtained through the matriarchal line would concur with the interpretation of an account in the Torino papyri, developed later in the present study. The lineage would then not hold the priesthood but be banned from it. Now, **Abraham does not say that Pharaoh belonged to a lineage which did not hold the priesthood, he clarifies that he belonged to a lineage through** *which he could not have the right of Priesthood.*

According to the syllogism, the ban is due to some act committed by Cham. Did Abraham mention which one? He mentions Cham's wife as follows: « *Égyptus, which in the Chaldean signifies Egypt, which signifies that which is forbidden* ». This passage does not make any sense at this point in the text if it does not have anything to do with the idea which it develops. Very frequently in the scriptures one finds names given to people at birth or as nicknames to underscore an event, a character trait or a particular feature. Thus Jacob's name was changed to Israel, meaning *one who fought with God*. On the opposite, Nimrod means *one who rebelled*. Egyptus, Abraham said, means *that which is forbidden*. Why say here it? If one considers it insignificant and meaningless, then it has no place here. But if it gives the reason why Pharaoh was banned from the priesthood, then it is exactly in the right paragraph. And, as we saw in the last chapter, the cause for the loss of the priesthood for a whole posterity is precisely a forbidden marriage.

So it was Cham's marriage which banned his descendants from the priesthood. Abraham explains it clearly in a few verses.

But how could Cain's lineage loose the right to hold the priesthood?

II
HOW CAIN'S LINEAGE
LOST THE PRIESTHOOD

Brigham Young explained that Cain's lineage lost the priesthood because of Abel's murder (1). It is certainly only the emerging part of the iceberg. Cain's descendants were even more wicked than their ancestor (2).

1
Abel's murder

Abel's murder by Cain is reported both in the Book of Genesis[89] and in the Book of Moses[90]. The story is known: Adam had many sons, among whom Cain and Abel. Abel became a shepherd and kept the commandments diligently. Cain became a ground tiller and took liberties with the commandments. The Lord instructed Adam to offer the firstlings of his flocks in sacrifice as a similitude of the sacrifice to come of the Only-begotten of the Father. Cain, no doubt informed of it, decided to offer the fruits of the earth which he had harvested. As a result of his disobedience, God looked with disfavor at his offering and warned him. Instead of repenting, Cain became angry. Jealous of his brother, seeing his flocks, he premeditated his crime. He made a covenant with Satan thinking that he could kill his brother without being discovered. But God would know it. After the murder, the earth was cursed for Cain, who was condemned to wander. He left with his wife, the daughter of one of his brothers, and several of Adam's children and grand-children, for another region further east.

Cain's sin is all the more serious as he had received great favors from God. Joseph Fielding Smith commented: « *Cain's great sin was not committed in ignorance. We have every reason to believe that he had the privilege of standing in the presence of messengers from heaven. In fact the scriptures infer that he was blessed by communication with the Father and was instructed by messengers from his presence. No doubt he held the Priesthood; otherwise his sin could not make of him Perdition. He sinned against the light. And this he did, so we are told, because he loved Satan more than he loved God*[91] ».

Beside the seriousness of the crime, the scripture reports Cain's lie when God asked him where his brother was. Believing, as he had been promised by Satan, that his sin would not be known, Cain answered that he did not know and added: « *Am I my brother's keeper?*[92] ». As a priesthood holder, Cain had become his brother's keeper. The prophet Ezekiel received the following reproof for the priesthood holders of his time: « *And the word of the Lord came unto me, saying: Son of man, prophesy against the shepherds of Israel! [...] Ye eat the fat, and ye clothe you with the wool, ye kill them that are fed: but ye feed not the flock. The diseased have ye not strengthened, neither have ye healed that which was sick, neither have ye bound up that which was broken, neither have ye brought again that which was driven away, neither have ye sought that which was lost[93]* ». **By acting as he did, Cain proved himself unworthy of the priesthood which he held.**

His descendants did worse.

2
Cain's descendants' behavior

Cain's descendants became even more wicked. The Book of Moses reports that Lemec killed Irad, unlike Cain not out of anger or to get gain, but because of an oath[94]. Wickeness then was not that of an isolated person anymore, but was organized in a group: « *from the days of Cain, there was a secret combination, and their works were in the dark [...]and their works were abominations [...]And thus the works of darkness began to prevail among all the sons of men[95]* » until they corrupted all of Adam's posterity, except for Noah's family, which retained the priesthood.

According to the Book of Moses, Cham also walked with God[96]. It was not without reason that

Pharaoh claimed that he was entitled to Noah's priesthood through Cham. It was because Cham had most certainly obtained it before his marriage. How did Cham's descendants react at being denied the priesthood?

CHAPTER 5

HOW'S CHAM'S POSTERITY REACTED

We would not be the first ones to feel unfairly treated if not granted equal blessings. We would find ourselves saying: Why am I not blessed? What have I done?

When not blessed, we react in different ways, depending on our understanding of the situation. We may:
- ➢ Either understand and accept that this may create a setting for a test,
- ➢ Or not understand but accept anyway by exercising faith, hoping that we will understand better someday,
- ➢ Or not understand, question and rebel.

Cham's immediate posterity decided to question the ban and to rebel. We will study their actions which are also additional evidences that there was, indeed, a ban (I). Later on, the open rebellion of the first descendants became more diffuse as many gods and forms of worships were created. The descendants were no longer rebelling; they were led astray by their fathers' traditions. We will attempt to take an overview of the people affected by the ban (II).

I
HOW CHAM'S IMMEDIATE POSTERITY REACTED

The scriptures teach that Cham was a righteous man: « *And thus Noah found grace in the eyes of the Lord; for Noah was a just man, and perfect in his generation; and he walked with God, as did also his three sons, Shem, Ham, and Japheth*[97] ». There is no doubt that he held the priesthood and that his posterity also claimed it from him: « *Pharaoh being of that lineage by which he could not have the right of Priesthood, notwithstanding the Pharaohs would fain claim it from Noah, through Ham*[98] ».

Cham's descendants refused to recognize the ban resulting for a mere marriage and claimed Cham's priesthood. They questioned the priesthood holders' decisions (1), used subterfuges to try and obtain the priesthood (2) and created a parallel authority (3).

1
Challenging priesthood decisions

Genesis reports that in the year when Peleg was born, around 2247 B.C., the earth was divided between the sons of Noah: « *And unto Eber were born two sons: the name of one was Peleg; for in his days was the earth divided [...]*[99] ».

The Book of Jubilees details how the division was made. It says that it was Noah who divided the earth between his three sons. Cham's share went: « *beyond the Gihon towards the south [...],extended towards the west till it reach[ed] the sea of Ma'uk [...],towards the north to the limits of Gadir [...]* ». Cham then divided this part between his sons: « *and the first portion came forth for Cush towards the east, and to the west of him for Mizraïm, and to the west of him for Put, and to the west of him on the sea for Canaan*[100] ».

The Book of Jubilees mentions an oath taken by Noah's sons and grandsons on the day the division was made, by which each committed himself to stay within the territory which had been allotted to him: « *And thus the sons of Noah divided unto their sons in the presence of Noah their father, and he bound them all by an oath, imprecating a curse on every one that sought to seize the portion which had not fallen (to him) by his lot. And they all said, 'So be it; so be it' for themselves and their sons forever throughout their generations [...]*[101] ».

In spite of his oath, Canaan disobeyed: « *And Canaan saw the land of Lebanon to the river of Egypt, that it was very good, and he went not into the land of his inheritance [...].And Ham, his father, and Cush and Mizraïm his brothers said unto him: 'Thou hast settled in a land which is not thine, and which did not fall to us by lot: do not do so; for if thou dost do so, thou and thy sons will fall in the land and (be) accursed through sedition; for by sedition ye have settled, and by sedition will thy children fall, and thou shalt be rooted out for ever. Dwell not in the dwelling of Shem; for to Shem and to his sons did it come by their lot. Cursed art thou, and cursed shalt thou be beyond all the sons of Noah, by the curse by which we bound ourselves by an oath in the presence of the holy judge, and in the presence of Noah our father. But he did not harken unto them, and dwelt in the land of Lebanon from Hamath to the entering of Egypt, he and his sons until this day. And for this reason that land is named Canaan*[102] ».

Canaan brought upon himself the curse announced by his grand-father. In the next paragraph, we will see a passage from Genesis which reports that Cham stole the priesthood garments. When he woke up, Noah strangely cursed Canaan instead of Cham. Two different acts of rebellion had probably taken place. Canaan had nothing to do with the stealth of the garments. His act of rebellion was to break his oath and to take possession of lands which had not been allotted to him. As a result, Canaan was cursed and his posterity will not be able to live in peace in the illegally occupied country. A prediction was made to his posterity that it will be forever uprooted, that it will suffer revolts, wars and slavery should it continue in its rebellion.

2
Subterfuges used to obtain recognition of the priesthood held

The Book of Jasher reports that Cham stole garments from Noah: « *And the garments of skin which God made for Adam and his wife, when they went out of the garden, were given to Cush. For after the death of Adam and his wife, the garments were given to Enoch, the son of Jared, and when Enoch was taken up to God, he gave them to Methuselah, his son. And at the death of Methuselah, Noah took them and brought them to the ark, and they were with him until he went out of the ark. And in their going out, Ham stole those garments from Noah his father, and he took them and hid them from his brothers. And when Ham begat his first born Cush, he gave him the garments in secret, and they were with Cush many days. And Cush also concealed them from his sons and brothers, and when Cush had begotten Nimrod, he gave him those garments through his love for him, and Nimrod grew up, and when he was twenty years old he put on those garments [...]*[103] ».

Members of the Church of Jesus Christ who participated in the temple endowment ceremony wear a priesthood garment, which represents the clothing of skin which the Lord made for Adam and Eve after the Fall.

Is it the same incident which made Noah naked under his tent one night[104]? Many hypotheses have been proposed as to what really transpired in Noah's tent while he was drunk. Did Cham just see his father's nakedness? Did he commit incest? Did he castrate his father? Did he only steal his garments? Rabbi Eleazer teaches that the Hebrew word *erwath* used in the scriptural passage does not refer to Noah's nakedness. In its original sense, it means covering of skin. So, Cham did not see his father's nakedness but his father's clothing of skin and stole it from him[105].

He did not steal the clothing because of its beauty but because of what it represented: the priesthood, authority, and power. According to the Talmud, Nimrod, Cham's grandson, was able to claim to have the power to govern the whole earth because he owned this garment, and wearing it was also the reason for his great success at hunting[106].

Cush's posterity was not the only one to claim the priesthood by using a subterfuge. Mizraïm's posterity did also. Let us recall that the pharaohs claimed it: « *Pharaoh being of that lineage by which he could not have the right of Priesthood, notwithstanding the Pharaohs would fain claim it from Noah, through Ham* ». Why through Cham? How could they obtain it from him while he could not pass it on? When did they believe that they had obtained it?

Some characters of the Egyptian mythology can also be compared to our ancestors, Noah and his immediate posterity. Noah and his wife would thus be Shou and Tefnout, the first sexually differentiated couple in the Egyptian mythology. Cham and Naama or Egyptus (mother) would be the god Ra and the goddess Nout. Finally, Mizraïm and Egyptus (daughter) would be Isis and Osiris, brother and sister in the mythology as well as in reality. If we hold to his representation as Osiris, Mizraïm must have died at a relatively young age. Egyptus wanted to settle her sons on the throne: « *When this woman discovered the land it was under water, who afterward settled her sons in it* ». She wanted them to hold the priesthood in order to legitimize their positions.

One of the Torino papyri, translated in 1883 by egyptologist Eugène Lefébure (1838-1908), tells the history summarized here: When Ra was still living on the earth, among the humans, he started to become senile. Isis, who coveted his power, placed a venomous snake on his way, which bit him. **She then waited till he was weak and feverish then**

she asked him to give her his secret name. Ra first lied to her but when pain became unbearable, he gave her the name in order to be healed[107].

For Egyptians, one's secret name represents one's power. Again according to mythology, Isis used it to bring Osiris back to life and to enable him to become the god of the hereafter, and to heal his son, Horus, from the many wounds caused by his brother and rival, Seth. What power can heal, resurrect and lead? The priesthood.

It may be that Naama (daughter) took advantage of her father Cham's senility to ask him to confer the priesthood to her or to her son, even though Cham could not pass it on.

3
Creation of a parallel authority

Claiming a priesthood which they did not possess, Cham's immediate descendants then created another one. At first, it looked similar to the true one, but it deviated, while retaining some striking similarities.

To understand this, all one has to do is read what Albert Mackey (1807-1881) wrote in the *Encyclopedia of freemasonry* under **Spurious Freemasonry**. The reader should replace « freemasonry » with « priesthood » in order to discover many components of the history of the

priesthood and of how the parallel authority came
into being:

« *For this term [spurious freemasonry], and for the
theory connected with it, we are indebted to Doctor
Oliver, whose speculations led him to the
conclusion that in the earliest ages of the world
there were two systems of Freemasonry, the one of
which, preserved by the patriarchs and their
descendants, he called Primitive or Pure
freemasonry.*

*The other, which was a schism from this system, he
designated as the Spurious Freemasonry of
Antiquity. To comprehend this system of Oliver, and
to understand his doctrine of the declension of the
Spurious from the Primitive Freemasonry, we must
remember that there were two races of men
descended from the loins of Adam, whose history is
as different as their characters were dissimilar.
There was the virtuous race of Seth and his
descendants, and the wicked one of Cain. Seth and
his children, down to Noah, preserved the dogmas
and instructions, the legends and symbols, which
had been received from their common progenitor,
Adam; but Cain and his descendants whose vices at
length brought on the destruction of the earth,
either totally forgot or greatly corrupted them.*

*Their Freemasonry was not the same as that of the
Sethite. They distorted the truth, and varied the
landmarks to suit their own profane purposes. At
length the two races became blended together. The
descendants of Seth, becoming corrupted by their
frequent communications with those of Cain,*

65

adopted their manners, and soon lost the principles of the Primitive Freemasonry, which at length were confined to Noah and his three sons, who alone, in the destruction of a wicked world, were thought worthy of receiving mercy.

Noah consequently preserved this system, and was the medium of communicating it to the post-diluvian world. Hence, immediately after the Deluge, Primitive Freemasonry was the only system extant. But this happy state of affairs was not to last. Ham, the son of Noah, who had been accursed by his father for his wickedness, had been long familiar with the corruptions of the system of Cain, and with the gradual deviations from truth which, through the influence or evil example, had crept into the system of Seth. After the Deluge, he propagated the worst features of both systems among his immediate descendants.

Two sets or parties, so to speak, now arose in the world - one which preserved the great truths of religion, and consequently of Freemasonry, which had been handed down from Adam, Enoch, and Noah - and another which deviated more and more from this pure, original Source. On the dispersion at the Tower of Babel, the schism became still wider and more irreconcilable. The legends of Primitive Freemasonry were altered, and its symbols perverted to a false worship; the mysteries were dedicated to the worship of false gods amid the practice of idolatrous rites, and in the place of the Pure or Primitive Freemasonry which continued to be cultivated among the patriarchal descendants of Noah, was established those

Mysteries of Paganism to which Doctor Oliver has given the name of the Spurious Freemasonry.

It is not to Doctor Oliver, nor to any very modern writer, that we are indebted for the idea of a Masonic schism in this early age of the world. The doctrine that Freemasonry was lost, that is to say, lost in its purity, to the larger portion of mankind, at the Tower of Babel, is still preserved in the ritual of Ancient Craft Masonry.

And in the Degree of Noachites, a Degree which is attached to the Scottish Rite, the fact is plainly adverted to as, indeed, the very foundation of the Degree. Two races of Freemasons are there distinctly named, the Noachites and the Hiramites; the former were the Conservators of the Primitive Freemasonry as the descendants of Noah; the latter were the descendants of Hiram, who was himself of the race which had fallen into Spurious Freemasonry, but had reunited himself to the true sect at the building of King Solomon's Temple, as we shall hereafter see. But the inventors of the Degree do not seem to have had any very precise notions in relation to this latter part of the history. The Mysteries, which constituted what has been thus called Spurious Freemasonry, were all more or less identical in character.

Varying in a few unimportant particulars, attributable to the influence of local causes, their great similarity in all important points showed their derivation from a common origin. In the first place, they were communicated through a system of initiation, by which the aspirant was gradually

prepared for the reception of their final doctrines;
the rites were performed at night, and in the most
retired situations, in caverns or amid the deep
recesses of groves and forests; and the secrets were
only communicated to the initiated after the
administration of an obligation.

Thus, Firmicus, a Latin author in the reign of
Constantine who about the year 346 A.D. wrote of
false objects of worship in De erroribus
profanarum religionum (book vii), tells us that
"when Orpheus explained the ceremonies of his
mysteries to candidates, he demanded of them, at
the very entrance, an oath, under the solemn
sanction of religion, that they would not betray the
rites to profane ears." Hence, as Warburton says
from Horus Apollo, the Egyptian hieroglyphic for
the mysteries was a grasshopper, because that
insect was supposed to have no mouth.

The ceremonies were all of a funereal character
commencing in representations of a lugubrious
description, they celebrated the legend of the death
and burial of some mythical being who was the
special object of their love and adoration. But these
rites thus beginning in lamentation, and typical of
death, always ended in joy. The object of their
sorrow was restored to life and immortality, and
the latter part of the ceremonial was descriptive of
his resurrection. Hence, the great doctrines of the
mysteries were the immortality of the soul and the
existence of a God.

Such, then, is the theory on the subject of what is
called Spurious Freemasonry, as taught by Doctor

Oliver and the disciples of his school. Primitive Freemasonry consisted of that traditional knowledge and symbolic instruction which had been handed down from Adam, through Enoch, Noah, and the rest of the patriarchs, to the time of Solomon. Spurious Freemasonry consisted of the doctrines and initiations practiced at first by the antediluvian descendants of Cain, and, after the dispersion at Babel, by the Pagan priests and philosophers in their Mysteries[108] ».

It is not surprising that, to some authors, the origin of current freemasonry can be traced back to Cham's immediate posterity. The Egypt of the Pharaohs is riddled with masonic references, so much so that Doctor Isindag wrote: « *Freemasonry is a social and ritual organization whose beginnings go back to Ancient Egypt[109] ».*

Accounts by freemason historians point to the same direction and show that Cain's and then Cham's lineages lost the right to hold the original priesthood and, in reaction, created a parallel priesthood. Patterned after the true one, it had no real authority and later became totally corrupted in the pursuit of local purposes.

Albert Mackey writes that the schism of freemasonries is mentioned in the basic initiatory ritual as well as in the Noachite degree which deals specifically with it. According to freemason historians, this schism did take place, as is evidenced by the similarities between the two freemasonries: ceremonies representing the death then the resurrection of the adored being, thus

69

recognizing the immortality of the soul and the existence of a God. These systems were comprised of an initiation, teachings and the making of commitments after the taking of an oath of confidentiality.

Freemason authors write about a meeting of both free-masonries at the time Solomon's temple was being built. They acknowledge that Hiram descended from the lineage which held the corrupted freemasonry but claim that he received the true freemasonry from Solomon for himself and his lineage in some vague circumstances.

The similarities between the pure and the corrupted freemasonries remind both of the ordinance of baptism, a symbol of Christ's burial and resurrection, and of the endowment and its initiatory system comprised of teachings and covenants. Some authors point to the differences between the priesthood and freemasonry and minimize the similarities out of fear that some people might think that Joseph Smith copied freemasonry[110]. That there should be similarities is normal: **it is freemasonry which copied the original priesthood**. By the way, it is as normal to find similarities in the rituals of the Christian Orthodox Church, in which also are to be found remnants of the original priesthood[111] taught by Christ after his resurrection[112]. Orthodox, Freemasons or Mormons, none of them copied the others but all of them have as a reference the original priesthood, altered by the two former, and restored by the latter.

Joseph Smith himself showed great clear-sightedness on this topic. Shortly after he was initiated into freemasonry and became a master in just two days, on March 15 and 16 March 1842, he stated in a letter dated June 17 1842: « *Masonry was taken from Priesthood but has become degenerated. But many things are perfect*[113] ».

Contrary to what freemasonry claims, there never was a reunification of the priesthood in Solomon's time. Hiram belonged to the lineage banned from the priesthood. Solomon himself never held it. The two main master masons could neither hold the original priesthood nor pass it on.

Today, key elements of the corrupted priesthood are found in the current freemasonry. Here are two which leave no doubt as to what the founders intended:

Tubal-Cain, on whom a great emphasis is placed in the freemasonic initiation. He belonged to Cain's lineage and held the corrupted priesthood.

Further, the oath taken by one entering freemasonry is the *oath of Nimrod*[114]. Nimrod is the very symbol of rebellion against God. The scriptures say that he was a valiant hunter before the Lord, a phrase to be taken in its derogatory meaning[115]. He rebelled openly against God, he built the Babel tower to defy Him[116], and he obtained and wore the priesthood garments stolen from Noah by Cham. He is the opposite example to the patriarchs Adam, Noah, Sem and Abraham. He descends from Cham and is one of the founders of this corrupted priesthood after the Flood.

II
CHAM'S POSTERITY

Nimrod rebelled openly against God, as did his contemporaries. The following generations did not do it as much. With the passing of time, the posterity was not in open rebellion any longer, it was misled by the traditions of the fathers. We will try to give an overview of the people belonging to Cham's lineage.

To apply the ban, the Church, of course, based its decisions on the most visible part of Cham's lineage, the black Africans, but it applied it also to all the individuals whose patriarchal blessing revealed that they belong to this lineage. For example, Church patriarch and General Authority, Eldred Gee Smith (1907-2013) once said: « *I had a young lady who was blond, a[n]d no sign or indications visibly of the Negro line at all, but yet she was deprived of going to the Temple...We have these conditions by the thousands in the United States today and are getting more of them*[117] **».**

Let us try and see who were Cham's children (1) and what marriage covenants they made (2). We will also see the look-alike situations which are not affected by the ban, as well as the exceptions, individuals who should have been affected but were not (3).

1
Cham's children

Cham's children and grandchildren seem to have respected their oaths and, except for Canaan, their territorial allotments made at the time the earth was divided by Noah among his sons.

At the time the earth divided, Cham was living in Kish, Mesopotamia, in what is Iraq today, about 10 miles south of Babylon. He went south and settled in Egypt, a country which the Bible calls « *Cham's country* » and which is called *Khem* in Egyptian.

As to his children, we know something of their geographical spread from Flavius Josephus's *The antiquities of the Jews*[118] written during the first century after A.D.

Mizraïm followed Cham. He also went south to Egypt. The Hebrew word for Egypt is *Mizraïm*. Flavius Josephus wrote : « *The memory also of the Mesraites is preserved in their name; for all we who inhabit this country called Egypt Mestre, and the Egyptians Mestreans [...]Now all the children of Mesraim, being eight in number, possessed the country from Gaza to Egypt, though it retained the name of one only, the Philistim [...]As for the rest, Ludieim, and Enemim, and Labim, who alone inhabited in Libya, and called the country from himself, Nedim, and Phethrosim, and Chesloim, and Cephthorim, we know nothing of them besides their names; for the Ethiopic war [...]was the cause that those cities were overthrown* ».

About Chous, Flavius Josephus wrote: « *Time has not at all hurt the name of Chus; for the Ethiopians, over whom he reigned, are even at this day, both by themselves and by all men in Asia, called Chusites [...] The children of these were these : Sabas, who founded the Sabeans; Evilas, who founded the Evileans, who are called Getuli; Sabathes founded the Sabathens, they are now called by the Greeks Astaborans; Sabactas settled the Sabactens; and Ragmus the Ragmeans; and he had two sons, the one of whom, Judadas, settled the Judadeans, a nation of the western Ethiopians, and left them his name; as did Sabas to the Sabeans: but Nimrod, the son of Chus, staid and tyrannized at Babylon* ».

Flavius Josephus wrote further: « *[Phout] was the founder of Libya, and called the inhabitants Phutites, from himself: there is also a river in the country of Moors which bears that name; whence it is that we may see the greatest part of the Grecian historiographers mention that river and the adjoining country by the name Phut: but the name it has now has been by change given it from one of the sons of Mesraim, who was called Lybyos* ».

Regarding Canaan, Flavius Josephus mentioned : « *[He] inhabited the country now called Judea, and called it from his own name Canaan [...]The sons of Canaan were these: Sidonius, who also built a city of the same name; it is called by the Greeks*

74

"Sidon" Amathus inhabited in Amathine, which is even now called "Amathe" by the inhabitants, although the Macedonians named it "Epiphania", from one of his posterity: Arudeus possessed the island Aradus: Arucas possessed Arce, which is in Libanus. But for the seven others, [Eueus,] Chetteus, Jebuseus, Amorreus, Gergesus, Eudeus, Sineus, Samareus, we have nothing in the sacred books but their names, for the Hebrews overthrew their cities ».

Flavius Joseph locates Sem and Japhet's descendants, Cham's brothers, in Asia and Europe, **which, as a consequence, puts black Africans among Cham's descendants**.

Maybe Genetics will someday clarify this topic. For now, it is too early to compare genetic populations to Biblical history. We will restrict ourselves to two remarks. First, the Church considered that the Dravidians from India and the Australian Aborigines were not under the ban since they belonged to a different lineage. Genetic studies classify these populations in very different male haplogroups: black Africans mainly in the haplogroup E, Australian Aborigines in haplogroup C, and Dravidians from India in haplogroup H. Therefore, they do not all necessarily descend from Cham. Second, black Africans are not the only ones who belong to haplogroup E. In this group are also characters such as Napoleon Bonaparte, William Harvey, the Wright brothers, Lyndon B. Johnson and Albert Einstein. If haplogroup E were comprised only of descendants from Cham, all these people and lineages would have no right to the priesthood. By far, Cham's lineage is not limited to black Africans. With the intermingling of populations, many people from all countries must have some of Cham's blood among their ancestors, which makes it harder to maintain the ban.

2
Covenants

The direct posterity was not the only one affected by the ban. It extended to the posterity of the people who married into it. Several great biblical characters contracted such marriages.

Abraham got Ismael from Agar, an Egyptian. Ismael and his posterity did not receive the priesthood. The Abrahamic covenant continues in Isaac's posterity but not in Ismael's[119].

Esaü married two hittite women, from Canaan's lineage, Adan and Oholibama, and one of Ismael's daughters, Basmath[120]. The covenant continues through Jacob's posterity, but not through Esau's posterity.

3
Deceiving appearances and exceptions

Critics of the lineage theory argue that some people whom they believe to descend from Cham are found among the ancestors of some priesthood holders. Among them: Juda's wife (a daughter of Shua, the Canaanite), Joseph's wife (Assenah), Eleazar's wife (one of Putiel's daughters) and Solomon's wife, Rahab, Booz's mother within Christ's very lineage[121].

For each of these cases, those critics admit that there exist contrary arguments, but they do not give them credit: Putiel would be another of Jethro's names, which would bring Eleazar's marriage back into the family[122]; Joseph was taken to Egypt during the reign of the Hyksos, which were of Semitic descent, maybe even of Hebrew ascendancy, which takes Assenah out of Cham's lineage[123]; the Rahab in Christ's lineage could not be the Jericho prostitute, who was several decades older and whose name should be translated as Rakhab instead of Rahab[124]; Finally, regarding Shua, the term Canaanite may refer as much to someone from Canaan's lineage as to someone living in the land of Canaan, or to a merchant[125].

In any event, if faced with a true case of priesthood holder from a lineage who had no right to receive it, we could put forth the argument of extreme faith. Ambrose of Milan (339-394) mentions that Ruth, the Moabite, who did not belong to Cham's lineage, was however a foreigner, whom a Jew could not marry, according to Deuteronomy 7: 3. He points out that she is however mentioned in Christ's lineage because, as the Bible explains: « *the law is not made for a righteous man, but for the lawless and disobedient*[126] ». Thus, through her great faith, Ruth would have been freed from the limitations of the Law[127].

And what about Cham's descendants who obtained the priesthood under Joseph Smith's presidency, Elijah Abel, Joseph T. Ball, Walker Lewis, Samuel Chambers and Edward Leggroan, to name but a few? True, for them, another argument can be considered: the revelation had not been received by Brigham Young, yet, and so the ban had not yet been reinstated. We believe in continuing revelation; we do not believe that all was restored by Joseph Smith and that no revelation can be received thereafter. The revelation process is closely related to the problems of a given time and to the prayers offered by the prophets in order to receive God's counsel on these subjects. Elijah Abel was ordained an elder on March 3rd 1836, before the question was asked or the answer given. Maybe he would not have been ordained, had the question arisen immediately after the restoration of the Gospel.

But maybe he would have been ordained because of his great faith, comparable to Ruth's. One very important aspect which should be emphasized is that, once the priesthood is received, the exception does not apply only to the holder; on the contrary, his descendants are the beneficiaries of it also. Enoch, Elijah Abel's son, was ordained an elder on November 27th 1900, and Elijah, his grandson was ordained on September 29th 1935[128]. So, both were ordained at a time when the ban was in force. Even in the exception, do we find the lineage principle.

Maybe it was this great faith, not of a few people but of many, which helped lift the ban before the time announced by Brigham Young.

CHAPTER 6

BAN WAIVERS BY ADOPTION

Nowadays, everybody focuses on the priesthood ban which affected Cham's lineage because it was the one which lasted the longest. It should not make us overlook, however, the priesthood and baptism bans which affected most lineages for centuries. Noah had three sons. What became of the right to hold the priesthood among the lineages descending from Japhet? The descendants of Gomer, Magog, Madaï, Javan, Tubal, Méschec and Tiras did not hold the priesthood in Christ's time and those of the people of Israel who held it could not pass it on if they married women descending from one of these forbidden lineages. What became of the right to hold the priesthood among the lineages descending from Sem? The descendants of Elam, Assur, Lud and Aram did not hold the priesthood in Christ's time and those of the people of Israel who held it could not pass it on if they married women descending from one of these lineages. **Sem, Cham, and Japhet had together a total of 16 sons. Only one of them, Arpacschad, had descendants who held the priesthood in Christ's time and they had to marry within their family in order to be able to pass their priesthood on to their descendants.**

The preceding chapters studied why Cham's lineage had lost the right to hold the priesthood and how Cham's posterity reacted to this. Even though we can only make assumptions about some developments, we can identify what happened in this lineage. **If the proper documentation were available, we would no doubt have much to say about the other lineages descending from Noah's**

sons, who, like Cham's lineage, no longer had the right to hold the priesthood in Christ's time.

Let us see now how baptism and the priesthood became available to these lineages.

The Scriptures tell twice of a call extended to the twelve apostles to go on a mission. The first one took place during the Savior's earthly ministry, the second one after his resurrection. During his earthly ministry, Christ gave the following direction to his apostles: « *Go not into the way of the Gentiles, and into any city of the Samaritans enter ye not: But go rather to the lost sheep of the house of Israel*[129] ». As we have already mentioned, he himself had received the same direction from his Father: « *I am not sent but unto the lost sheep of the house of Israel*[130] ». After his resurrection, the assignment changed: « *Go ye therefore, and teach all nations, baptizing them in the name of the Father, and of the Son, and of the Holy Ghost*[131] ».

This could lead us to believe that the ban concerning certain lineages was thus lifted and that the privilege of the house of Israel to receive the Gospel being now extended to all and that all also had a right to hold the priesthood. The heathens were allowed to be baptized. This however is false. Paul taught that, through baptism, one is adopted into Abraham's lineage and thus becomes heir to the promises: « *For as many of you as have been baptized into Christ have put on Christ [...]And if ye be Christ's, then are ye Abraham's seed, and heirs according to the promise*[132] ».

81

People who are baptized do not inherit promises because of their original lineage but because of Abraham, Isaac and Jacob's lineage into which they are adopted, being linked to one of the twelve tribes of Israel. Through this adoption, they are to inherit all of Abraham's blessings which we have already studied: a land, a posterity, the Gospel and the right to hold the priesthood. **Why then were Cham's descendants the only ones to be denied access to the priesthood because of the original lineage in spite of their being adopted?** Why did God decide to grant a progressive restoration of the blessings promised to Abraham for Cham's posterity, first access to the Gospel through baptism, in Peter's time then access to the priesthood in 1978?

Brigham Young gave a justification. **He taught that Cham's posterity would also receive the blessings in due time but that time had not come yet because the first will be the last**: « *They [The descendants of Cain/Ham] never can hold the Priesthood or share in it until all the other descendants of Adam have received the promises and enjoyed the blessings of the Priesthood and the keys thereof. Until the last ones of the residue of Adam's children are brought up to that favourable position, the children of Cain cannot receive the first ordinances of the Priesthood. They were the first that were cursed, and they will be the last from whom the curse will be removed. When the residue of the family of Adam come up and receive their blessings, then the curse will be removed from the seed of Cain, and they will receive blessings in like proportion*[133] ».

This notion that *the first shall be last and the last shall be first* makes reference to a passage of Scripture. This does not refer specifically to the priesthood but is a general statement for blessings. In Matthew, Mark and Luke's gospels, we read: « *Many that are first shall be last; and the last shall be first*[134]; *and, behold, there are last which shall be first, and there are first which shall be last*[135] ».

But how do you explain this notion that the first shall be last? Brigham Young interpreted his revelation as implying a lifting of the ban which would take place only after the resurrection, after all of Adam's other descendants would have received the blessings of the priesthood. Maybe it was only his personal interpretation of the revelation, maybe it was the way that he received it. This would not have been the first case of a ban lifted by a great faith. For example, Jesus healed the daughter of the Canaanite woman after reminding her that he had come only for the house of Israel[136]. He also healed the centurion's servant, thus justifying the exception: « *Verily I say unto you, I have not found so great faith, no, not in Israel*[137] ».

In his study *Spencer W. Kimball and the revelation on the priesthood*, Edward L. Kimball, details the abundant faith demonstrated by Cham's descendants in embracing the Gospel so fervently in spite of their being banned from the priesthood. He explains why the faith which they demonstrated led the prophets to ask the Lord about the end of the ban until the revelation obtained by Spencer W. Kimball in 1978. In the declaration, we read:

« *Aware of the promises made by the prophets and presidents of the Church who have preceded us that at some time, in God's eternal plan, all of our brethren who are worthy may receive the priesthood,* **and witnessing the faithfulness of those from whom the priesthood has been withheld**, *we have pleaded long and earnestly in behalf of these, our faithful brethren, spending many hours in the Upper Room of the Temple supplicating the Lord for divine guidance. He has heard our prayers, and by revelation has confirmed that the long-promised day has come when every faithful, worthy man in the Church may receive the holy priesthood [...]*[138] ».

There remains one last question: why is one born in one lineage rather than in another one? Even though Elder Oaks declares that « *It's not the pattern of the Lord to give reasons*[139] », some Church Authorities have attempted to justify the lineage criterion through the *theory of the less valiant*. Such explanation was erroneous but the question is still a legitimate one.

CHAPTER 7

GENERAL CONSIDERATIONS
ABOUT BLESSINGS
AND
THE RIGHT TIME
TO OBTAIN THEM

Holding the priesthood is not a right. It is a blessing from God and, as such, it is subject to all rules relating to blessings.

We will see their definition (I), the conditions to obtain them (II), the time to obtain them (III) and the reasons why their granting can be delayed (IV).

I
DEFINITION OF A BLESSING

The Guide to the Scriptures defines a blessing as the **fact that god** « *confers divine favor upon someone*[140] ».

There are all sorts of blessings:
- ➢ Spiritual gifts like feeling the Holy-Ghost, obtaining a testimony, a knowledge of the Gospel, holding the priesthood, accessing the ordinances necessary to our salvation, seeing God, obtaining eternal life.
- ➢ Physical blessings like giving life, being fruitful, being healthy.
- ➢ Intellectual gifts like acquiring easily and retaining all sorts of knowledge.
- ➢ Psychological rewards like having wisdom, feeling love, joy, peace, patience, goodness, benevolence, faithfulness, kindness and temperance.
- ➢ Material benefits like having a land, a home, prospering.

With this simple list, we see that **No one has all divine gifts.** Speaking about some of them, Paul taught that they are **allotted to everyone by God, according to his will, for the common good**[141]. This applies to all blessings. There is no automatic entitlement, no equality or parity between human beings.

II
OBEDIENCE, A REQUIREMENT
FOR BLESSINGS

When a blessing is not granted, we tend to look for the fault which prevents us from obtaining it. This is caused by a misunderstanding of how blessings are obtained.

In the *Doctrine and covenants*, we learn that, in order to obtain a blessing, one needs to obey the commandments: « *There is a law, irrevocably decreed in heaven before the foundations of this world, upon which all blessings are predicated - And when we obtain any blessing from God, it is by obedience to that law upon which it is predicated*[142] ».

Jehovah explained to Moses: « *Behold, I set before you this day a blessing and a curse; A blessing, if ye obey the commandments of the Lord your God, which I command you this day: And a curse, if ye will not obey the commandments of the Lord your God, but turn aside out of the way which I command you this day, to go after other gods, which ye have not known*[143] ».

The doctrine is clear: whether or not we obtain a blessing depends upon our obedience. For some blessings, we can even identify the related commandments, for example to live the Word of Wisdom carries the blessing to be healthy[144], reading the scriptures and acting according to what they say help us to be successful in our undertakings[145], the law of tithing offers the blessing of opening of the windows of heaven[146].

We then jump to the conclusion that, if we do not obtain a blessing, it is because of an act of disobedience.

We forget that **God decides when and which blessing will be granted. The blessing will be withheld only temporarily from the righteous**.

III
WHEN BLESSINGS ARE OBTAINED

Our society has greatly modified the perception of time. Formerly, it took a letter sent from across the world weeks or months to reach its destination. Now, an email covers the same distance in just a moment. We are not better than the man who bought seeds and then complained the next day that they still had not grown. We, too, expect immediate reward from God for our obedience.

A look at people's lives will show us that everything happens according to God's plan. So many worthy people cannot have children, are sick or did not know the Gospel during their lives. Conversely, many wicked people prosper.

The faithful will find some comfort and understanding in the words of the prophets. Lorenzo Snow (1814-1901) told people who cannot get married or have children: « *I desire to give a little explanation for the comfort and consolation of parties in this condition: there is no latter day saint who dies after having lived a faithful life who will lose anything because of having failed to do certain things when opportunities were not available to him or her. In other words **if a young man or a young woman has no opportunity of getting married and they live faithful lives up to the time of their death, they will have all the blessings, exaltation, and glory that any man or woman will have who had this opportunity and were faithful to their marriage covenants. This is sure and positive [...]***[147] ».

More generally speaking, the prophet Malachi reported the Lord's words as follows: « *Your words have been stout against me, saith the Lord. Yet ye say, What have we spoken so much against thee? Ye have said, It is vain to serve God: and what profit is it that we have kept his ordinance, and that we have walked mournfully before the Lord of hosts? And now we call the proud happy; yea, they that work wickedness are set up; yea, they that tempt God are even delivered. Then they that feared the Lord spake often one to another: and the Lord* *hearkened, and heard it, and a book of remembrance was written before him for them that feared the Lord, and that thought upon his name. And **they shall be mine**, saith the Lord of hosts, **in that day when I make up my jewels**; and I will spare them, as a man spareth his own son that serveth him. **Then shall ye return, and discern between the righteous and the wicked, between him that serveth God and him that serveth him not**[148] ».*

So, **the righteous may have to wait until the next life to obtain the blessings which they deserve through their obedience.** What are the justifications for this?

IV
REASONS WHY SOME BLESSINGS ARE DELAYED

How then do we explain that a righteous individual must wait until the next life to obtain a blessing?

The theory of the behavior in the premortal existence or the theory of the more and less valiant was first put forth. It provides answers which seem logical, but are erroneous (1). Its application shows its limits (2). Waiting for blessings is part of our test in mortality (3).

1
Introducing the erroneous theory of the behavior during the premortal existence

The theory of the behavior during the premortal existence is erroneous even though it is based on a reasoning which seems logical. It does not match however the fanciful extrapolations which get around about it.

The most exaggerated extrapolation stated that part of our Heavenly Father's children who came to earth took a neutral stand when Lucifer rebelled. It is just the opposite. It was B. H. Roberts' opinion (1857-1933) but he was careful to start his reasoning by « *I Think*[149] ». Official positions however, refuted any neutrality. In his book *The way of perfection*, Joseph Fielding Smith, immediately after B. H. Roberts's reasoning, quoted the Church's official position taught as early as Brigham Young's time: « *Lorenzo Snow asked if the spirits of negroes were neutral in heaven [...]. President Young said No they were not [...]*[150] ». In a letter addressed to Mr. M. Knudson, the First Presidency of the Church, under the direction of the prophet Joseph F. Smith, answered: « *There were no neutral spirits in heaven at the time of the rebellion*[151] ». All those who come to earth proved valiant before.

According to that theory however, people would have been valiant to different degrees, thus having the right to more or fewer blessings on the earth. This hypothesis was first used to explain why some people were chosen to belong to the elect people, favored by God to be the first to know the Gospel. Apostle Orson Pratt (1811-1881) spoke of: « *many spirits that are more noble, more intelligent than others*[152] » kept to be born into the Latter-day Saint families in our time. Today we still find some remnants of this teaching in institute manuals, which explains the birth into the Israelite lineage when it was the first to learn the Gospel[153]. In another manual, the argument of premortal valor is also put forth to explain the time, place and circumstances of our birth[154], as well as the callings to which we may have been pre-ordained[155].

But there can be more valiant spirits only if others were less so. The less valiant spirits would find themselves limited as regards the blessings that can be obtained on the earth.

The idea that blessings would be granted on earth based on our behavior is not totally groundless. Harold B. Lee (1899-1973) remarked: « *Each one of us will be judged when we leave this earth according to his or her deeds during our lives here in mortality. Isn't it just as reasonable to believe that what we have received here in this earth life was given to each of us according to the merits of our conduct before we came here?*[156] ». This reasoning, which seemed logical then, has now been dropped.

According to this theory, taken to its logical extreme, our earthly testing environment would depend on how valiant we were in the premortal existence. The most valiant would receive the greatest blessings. Thus, on the earth, the unrighteous would obtain a number of blessings because of their valiant behavior in the premortal existence. Similarly, blessings received on earth do not prejudge at all how valiant each one of us will prove and how he or she will be compensated for it in the hereafter.

This justification was once unanimously accepted. Cham's posterity's ban from the priesthood was viewed as an instance of delayed blessings. The First Presidency of the Church declared in 1949: « *The position of the Church [the ban of the priesthood] regarding the Negro may be understood when another doctrine of the Church is kept in mind, namely, that the conduct of spirits in the premortal existence has some determining effect upon the conditions and circumstances under which these spirits take on mortality*[157] ».

We must however be careful not to give these words a meaning which they do not have. True, they tell of a valor lesser than that of the people who have had the right to know the Gospel and to hold the priesthood. But regarding Cham's descendants who were able to accept the Gospel without holding the priesthood, the level of their valor is higher than the level of the valor of the vast majority of the people who came to earth, whatever the color of their skin.

2
The limits which discredit the theory of behavior during the premortal existence

According to this theory, the way the spirits behaved in the premortal existence would have had a determining impact on their conditions and circumstances in mortality. The degree of their valor would determine the number and nature of the blessings they could obtain on the earth. We would be losing some of these blessings now by misusing our free agency, for example, by rejecting the Gospel which was proclaimed to us.

Even though this theory has some consistency, its application discredits it. How do you identify one's degree of valor in the premortal existence based on one's earthly blessings? If there were only one criterion or if the order in which blessings are obtained were always the same, all that it would be taken into consideration, even though the use of the free agency on earth puts man below the qualifying level reached in the premortal existence. But we see that the blessings are of many kinds, that the ways they combine among human beings are infinite. How does one classify blessings? And to which acts does one associate which blessings? One can hold the priesthood and not be fruitful and vice and versa. Who is more blessed?

Joseph Fielding Smith had already started to minimize this theory: « *It is a reasonable thing to believe that the spirits of the premortal state were of varying degrees of intelligence and faithfulness. This thought is conveyed in many passages of scripture, such as Acts 17:24-27; Deuteronomy 32:8; Abraham 3:19-26. However, to dwell upon this topic and point out certain nations as having been cursed because of their acts in the pre-existence, enters too much on the realm of speculation. Therefore, let it suffice that the negro is barred from the Priesthood and the reason some day we may understand*[158] ».

Nowadays, this theory is not put forth any longer by the Church of Jesus Christ of Latter-day Saints: « *Over time, Church leaders and members advanced many theories to explain the priesthood and temple restrictions. None of these explanations is accepted today as the official doctrine of the Church*[159] ».

3
Man put to the test in the mortal condition

It is a very human tendency, and one not limited to our time, to look for a fault to explain why a blessing is not received. In Christ's time, when the apostles saw a man blind from birth, they could not help asking: « *Master, who did sin, this man, or his parents, that he was born blind?*[160] », assuming that some sin had been committed during the premortal existence.

There is no hint of any sin or lack of valor in the Master's answer: « *Neither hath this man sinned, nor his parents: but that the works of God should be made manifest in him*[161] ».

Job was another person who was severely tried. He was first extremely blessed with a posterity, prosperity, health and a knowledge of God. Then he lost everything: his children, his wealth, his health, to the point where he wanted to die so as not to suffer anymore. He became even more afflicted when, here also, his friends believed that what had happened to him was the consequence of his and his family's sins: « *Doth God pervert judgment? or doth the Almighty pervert justice? If thy children have sinned against him, and he have cast them away for their transgression*[162] » [...] « *Will he reprove thee for fear of thee? will he enter with thee into judgment? Is not thy wickedness great? and thine iniquities infinite? For thou hast taken a pledge from thy brother for nought, and stripped the naked of their clothing. Thou hast not given water to the weary to drink, and thou hast withholden bread from the hungry. But as for the mighty man, he had the earth; and the honourable man dwelt in it. Thou hast sent widows away empty, and the arms of the fatherless have been broken. Therefore snares are round about thee, and sudden fear troubleth thee*[163] ».

Job's situation before his trials was just the opposite of what his friends had concluded: « *And the Lord said unto Satan, Hast thou considered my servant Job, that there is none like him in the earth, a perfect and an upright man, one that feareth God, and escheweth evil?*[164] ».

Amulek taught the purpose of our coming to earth: « *For behold, this life is the time for men to prepare to meet God; yea, behold the day of this life is the day for men to perform their labors*[165] ».

Abraham quoted Christ's words when he created the earth: « *We will go down, for there is space there, and we will take of these materials, and we will make an earth whereon these may dwell; and we will prove them herewith, to see if they will do all things whatsoever the Lord their God shall command them*[166] ».

James asked us to reconsider the purpose of our trials: « *My brethren, count it all joy when ye fall into various temptations; Knowing this, that the trying of your faith worketh patience. But let patience have her perfect work, that ye may be perfect and entire, wanting nothing*[167] ».

The circumstances in which we put on mortality, and obtain or do not obtain certain blessings here on earth, are an integral part of our being tested.

CONCLUSION

President Ezra Taft Benson said: « *There have been and continue to be attempts made to bring [a humanistic] philosophy into our own Church history. ... The emphasis is to underplay revelation and God's intervention in significant events and to inordinately humanize the prophets of God so that their human frailties become more apparent than their spiritual qualities*[168] ».

It is exactly the case with Brigham Young regarding the revelation which he received on the priesthood to maintain the ban on the grounds of lineage.

Critics of Brigham Young say loud and clear that he allowed himself to be influence by local opinions, that the priesthood ban is linked to the racist theories which developed during the 17th and 18th centuries. We have demonstrated that this is false. We have recalled that Brigham Young linked the ban to marriage and we have shown, using ancient writings, that he was right. By not marrying within his family, Cham deprived his descendants from the right to hold the priesthood.

Brigham Young was a prophet of God, as was Joseph Smith, which is confirmed by his whole life and all his teachings. Granted, some of what he said could be named racist today but his revelation is absolutely not.

To the author's knowledge, up to now, no study has made the effort of looking into the issue of lineage. All previous efforts stopped at the foggy racist theories of the 17th and 18th centuries preferring, at best, to hold to the official position « *We don't know* » or, at worst, to say that it was a mistake made and perpetuated by our modern prophets under the influence of the beliefs of their time.

At the end of this study, we express our hope that others will search beyond appearances to prove better than we have been able to do, that Brigham Young was speaking under divine inspiration when he stated the revelation that linked the priesthood ban to lineage.

[1] *Pearl of Great Price*, Official Declaration n°2.

[2] *Race and the Priesthood*, lds.org

[3] Interview with Jeffrey Holland, March 4th 2006.

[4] Dallin H. Oaks, Interview with Associated Press, in Daily Herald, Provo, Utah, 5 June 1988.

[5] Brigham Young's statement made during the Salt Lake City legislative session, Thursday February 5th 1852 as reported in Wilford Woodruff's journal (Wilford Woodruff's Journal, 1833-1898 Typescript, vol. 4, edited by Scott G. Kenney, Signature Books, pp. 97-99).

[6] French *Larousse* dictionary.

[7] Paul III's letter *Veritas Ipsa* June 2, 1537, to all Christians : « *Truth himself, who can neither deceive nor be deceived, clearly affirmed when he entrusted the preachers of the faith with the ministry of the word : « Go, teach all nations ». He said all, without exception, since all people are capable of receiving the teaching of faith. Perceiving this, the jealous enemy of the human race, ever hostile to human works in order to destroy them, devised a new way of preventing that the word of God be proclaimed to the nations for their salvation. He influenced certain of his minions, anxious to satisfy their greed, to declare publicly that the inhabitants of the West and South Indies, and other peoples still unknown to us at that time, should be used for our service, like brute beasts, under the pretext that they did not know the Catholic faith. They reduced them to slavery by imposing on them a forced labour which they would scarcely have dared to impose on their own domestic animals. Now We who, despite our unworthiness, are the Lord's representative on earth and wish, with all our strength, to bring into his fold those who have been entrusted to us and who are still outside the sheepfold, consider that the Indians, as true human beings, are not only capable of accepting the Christian faith but even more, from what We have learned, run with haste to embrace this faith. And desiring to bring them all the help necessary, We decide and declare, by these letters, in virtue of Our Apostolic Authority, that the said Indians and all other peoples whom Christians might come to know, even if they live outside the faith, can freely and licitly use, possess and*

enjoy freedom and the possession of their goods, and must not be enslaved. Every measure which contradicts these principles is abrogated and invalid. Moreover, We decide and declare that the Indians and the other peoples must be invited to the said faith of Christ by the proclamation of the word of God and by the example of a virtuous life. All things past or future which are contrary to these regulations are to be considered null and void ». Translation taken from the book *The Emergence of Human Rights in Europe: An Anthology* published by Jean Carpentier p.153 et 154.

[8] Systema theologicum ex prae Adamitarum hypothesi. pars prima. 1655, posted on the website Gallica.

[9] Voltaire. 1734. *Treatise on Metaphysics*, chap. 1: « On the various species of men » : « *It seems to me that I am quite justified in believing that it is with men as with trees ; that pear trees, pines, oaks, and apricot trees do not come from the same tree, and that bearded white men, wooly haired black men, yellow men with manes, and beardless men do not come from the same man* ».

[10] « Samuel Georges Morton claimed that he could define the intellectual ability of a race by the skull capacity. A large volume meant a large brain and high intellectual capacity, and a small skull indicated a small brain and decreased intellectual capacity. He was reputed to hold the largest collection of skulls, on which he based his research. He claimed that each race had a separate origin, and that a descending order of intelligence could be discerned that placed Caucasians at the pinnacle and Negroes at the lowest point, with various other race groups in between ». Text from the wikipedia page on the author, quoting Bates, Crispin (1995). « *Race, Caste and Tribe in Central India: the early origins of Indian anthropometry* ». In Robb, Peter.*The Concept of Race in South Asia*. Delhi: Oxford University Press. p. 225. Retrieved 2011-11-30. ISBN 978-0-19-563767-0.

[11] For example, Abu-al-Qasim Sa`id ibn-Ahmad al-Andalusi (1029-1070), wrote in his book *On the History of Science* (Al-tarif bi-Tabaqat al-Umm): « *the air is burning hot and the climate outside is subtle. Thus the Sûdans' tempers flare and their humours get worked up; this is also the reason why their*

color is black and their hair frizzy. Hence any balance in judgment, any safety in appreciations are annihilated. With them, levity prevails and stupidity and ignorance dominate ».

[12] The Holy Bible (KJV), Acts 17: 26

[13] Paul de Lagarde, Materialien zur Kritik und Geschichte des Pentateuchs (Leipzig, 1867), part II.

[14] Iso' dadh of Merv's commentary on the Old Testament translated by C. van den Eynde. Series: Corpus scriptorum Christianorum Orientalium; v. 156. Scriptores syri, T. 75 (Louvain, 1955), p. 139.

[15] Sprengling and Graham, Barhebraeus' Scholia one the Old Testament, pp.40-41, to Gen 9:22

[16] Tryggve Kronholm, Motifs from Genesis 1-11, pp. 135-42

[17] The History off Abel and Cain, 10, in Lipscomb, The Armenian Apocryphal Adam Literature, pp. 145 and 250 for the text and 160 and 271 for the translation.

[18] The Holy Bible (KJV), Genesis 9: 25-27.

[19] Jean Louis Hannemann, Curiosum Scrutinium nigritudinis posterum Cham i.e. Aethiopum, edited by J. Reumann (1677), quoted in Patricia Gravatt, L'Eglise et l'esclavage, Paris, pub. L'Harmattan, 2003.

[20] After the Dutch, The Anglican Church followed suit via the Society for the Propagation of the Word in the faraway lands which had plantations in Barbados. Among the leaders of the Society, were the archbishop of Canterbury and the bishops of London and of York. When the slaves were emancipated, the Church was compensated for the loss of its slaves. Lastly, the Catholic Church did not rule on the justification itself, but let its local leaders fully adhere to the justification. As a consequence, during Vatican I (1869-1870), a group of 65 bishops approached the Pope with a postulatum asking him to lift the curse on the sons of Cham.

[21] Translation of Benjamin Braude in Cham et Noé. Race et esclavage entre judaïsme, christianisme et Islam. In : Annales. Histoire, Sciences sociales. 57ème année, N.1, 2002, pp.93-125, which translation differs from Louis Doutreleau's, pub. And translator of Origène, Homélie sur la Genèse, Paris, Le Cerf, 1976, pp. 374-375.

[22] Bruce R. McConkie, *The New Revelation on Priesthood*, in *Priesthood* (Salt Lake City: Deseret Book, 1981), pp. 126-37, esp. p. 128.

[23] Talk given on May 15th 1988 at a worldwide fireside celebrating the 159th anniversary of the restauration of the priesthood. Talk available at lds.org.

[24] *Pearl of Great Price, Article of faith* n°2.

[25] *The Holy Bible (KJV)*, Ezekiel 18: 20

[26] Edward L. Kimball *Spencer W. Kimball and the Revelation on Priesthood*, *BYU Studies 47*, n°2 (2008): 4-78.

[27] *The Book of Mormon*, 2 Nephi 27: 25 ; Mosiah 1: 5 ; Mosiah 10: 12 ; Alma 3: 8 ; Alma 9: 16-17 ; Alma 17: 5 ; Alma 19: 14 ; Alma 21: 17 ; Alma 23: 3 ; Alma 26: 24 ; Alma 37: 9 ; Alma 47: 36 ; Alma 56: 4 ; Alma 60: 32, Helaman 5: 19 and 51, Helaman 15: 4 and 15.

[28] *The Book of Mormon*, Alma 17: 15.

[29] *The Holy Bible (KJV)*, 1 Timothy 1: 4.

[30] *The Holy Bible (KJV)*, Titus 3: 9.

[31] *The Life and Teachings of Jesus Christ and His Apostles* 45-10.

[32] *The Holy Bible (KJV)*, Nehemiah 7: 64.

[33] *The Life and Teachings of Jesus Christ and His Apostles* 44-14.

[34] *The Holy Bible (KJV)*, Matthew 10: 5-6.

[35] *The Holy Bible (KJV)*, Matthew 15: 24.

[36] *The Holy Bible (KJV)*, Acts 13: 46.

[37] *The Holy Bible (KJV)*, Acts 10.

[38] *The Holy Bible (KJV)*, Galatians 3: 27-29.

[39] *Pearl of Great Price*, Abraham 2: 10.

[40] Joseph Fielding Smith, *Doctrine of Salvation*, Vol 3, p.220-221.

[41] John A. Widtsoe, *Evidences and Reconciliations*, p. 400

[42] *The Book of Mormon*, 2 Nephi 30: 1-2.

[43] *Doctrine and covenants* 113: 7-8.

[44] *The Holy Bible (KJV)*, Genesis 49.

[45] *The Holy Bible (KJV)*, Deuteronomy 33.

[46] *The Holy Bible (KJV)*, Genesis 17: 20-21.

[47] *The Holy Bible (KJV)*, Genesis 48: 15-20.

[48] *The Book of Mormon*, 2 Nephi 4: 3-10.

[49] *Pearl of Great Price*, Abraham 1: 26.

[50] *The Holy Bible (KJV)*, Genesis 17: 7.

[51] *The Holy Bible (KJV)*, Genesis 17: 5 and 15.

[52] *The Holy Bible (KJV)*, Genesis 17: 11-14.

[53] *The Holy Bible (KJV)*, Genesis 17: 1.

[54] *The Holy Bible (KJV)*, Isaiah 49: 16.

[55] *The Holy Bible (KJV)*, Isaiah 49: 15.

[56] *The Holy Bible (KJV)*, Matthew 23: 37.

[57] *The Holy Bible (KJV)*, Leviticus 26: 42-45.

[58] *The Holy Bible (KJV)*, Genesis 17: 8.

[59] *Pearl of Great Price*, Abraham 2: 6.

[60] *The Holy Bible (KJV)*, Genesis 17: 2 and 4.

[61] *Pearl of Great Price*, Abraham 1: 2 and 5.

[62] *Pearl of Great Price*, Abraham 1: 27.

[63] Also called Levi's Testament, found among the Qumrân Dead Sea Scrolls (1Q21; 4Q213-214b).

[64] Found among the Qumrân Dead Sea Scrolls (4Q200).

[65] *Aramaic Levi Document* 5: 7-8 et 6: 1-6.

[66] *Book of Tobit* 4: 12.

[67] *The Holy Bible (KJV)*, Genesis 17: 19-21.

[68] *The Holy Bible (KJV)*, Genesis 24: 2-4.

[69] *The Holy Bible (KJV)*, Genesis 28: 1-2.

[70] *The Holy Bible (KJV)*, Genesis 27: 46.

[71] Christine Hayes, *Gentile Impurities and Jewish Identities : Intermarriage and Conversion from the Bible to the Talmud,* Oxford University Press; 1 edition (November 14, 2002)

[72] *The Holy Bible (KJV)*, Ezra 9: 1.

[73] *The Holy Bible (KJV)*, Leviticus 21: 7.

[74] Kampen, *4QMMT and the New Testament Studies*, in *4QMMT: New Perspectives on Qumran Law and History* (ed. J. Kampen and M. J. Bernstein; SBL Symposium Series 2; Atlanta: Scholars Press, 1996).

[75] Josephus, *Against Apion* I : 7.

[76] Josephus, Against *Apion* I : 7.

[77] *The Holy Bible (KJV)*, Nehemiah 7: 64.

[78] *The Holy Bible (KJV)*, Ezra 10: 3.

[79] *Journal History of the Church*, February 13th 1849, Church History Library.

[80] *Pearl of Great Price*, Moses 7: 22.

[81] *Genesis Rabbah*, chapter 23.

[82] *The Holy Bible (KJV)*, Genesis 4: 22.

[83] *Book of Jasher* 5: 15.

[84] *The Holy Bible*, Joshua 10: 13 and 2 Samuel 1: 18.

[85] *Book of Tobit* 4: 12.

[86] Cumberland, *Sanchoniathon's History*, p. 107.

[87] *Pearl of Great Price*, Abraham 1: 21-27.

[88] Hugh Nibley, *Abraham in Egypt,* chapter 8 The sacrifice of Sarah.

[89] *The Holy Bible (KJV)*, Genesis 4: 1-16.

[90] *Pearl of Great Price*, Moses 16: 42

[91] Joseph Fielding Smith, *The way to perfection*, p.97-98.

[92] *The Holy Bible (KJV)*, Genesis 4: 9 and *Pearl of Great Price*, Moses 5: 34.

[93] *The Holy Bible (KJV)*, Ezekiel 34: 1-10.

[94] *Pearl of Great Price*, Moses 5: 50.

[95] *Pearl of Great Price*, Moses 5: 51, 52 and 55.

[96] *Pearl of Great Price*, Moses 8: 27.

[97] *Pearl of Great Price*, Moses 8: 27.

[98] *Pearl of Great Price*, Abraham 1: 27.

[99] *The Holy Bible (KJV)*, Genesis 10: 25.

[100] *Book of Jubilees* 8: 22 and 9: 1. Traduction from *The Apocrypha and Pseudepigrapha of the Old Testament* by R.H. Charles, Oxford: Clarendon Press, 1913 Edited by Joshua Williams, Northwest Nazarene College.

[101] *Book of Jubilees* 9: 15. Idem.

[102] *Book of Jubilees* 10: 29-34. Idem.

[103] *Book of Jasher* 7: 24-29, published by J. H. Parry & Company in Salt Lake City : 1887.

[104] *The Holy Bible (KJV)*, Genesis 9: 20-23.

[105] Quoted by Hugh Nibley in his book *Lehi in the desert,* chapter 1 The trouble Orient.

[106] Idem. Hugh Nibley cite *Nimrod*, JE 9 : 309-11 - Jeremias, Das Alte Testament im Lichte des Alten Orients, pp. 159-160.

[107] E. Lefebure, *Un chapitre de la chronique solaire*.

[108] Albert Mackey, *Encyclopedia of Freemasonry*.

[109] Dr Selami Isindag, *Sezerman Kardes VII, Masonlukta Yorumlama Vardir Ama Putlastirma Yoktur, Masonluktan Esinlenmeler*, Istanbul 1977, p.120.

[110] Matthew B. Brown, *Exploring the connection between mormons and masons*, Covenant Communications, Inc., 2009.

[111] Idem, Chapter 3: The origins of Masonic Practice – Masonic lodgdes imitate Christian Churches.

[112] S. Kent Brown et C. Wilfred Griggs *The 40-day Ministry*, Ensign August 1975

[113] Letter dated June 27, 1842, Church Archives.

[114] *Freemasonry today*, Spring 2006.

[115] The Hebrew word *liphné*, which translates literally as *to the face of*, can mean *against* or *in opposition to*. The Babylonian Talmud (Erouvin 53a) gives the same meaning: « *Why was he called Nimrod? Because in his reign he led the entire world in rebellion against himself [God]* ».

[116] Josephus, *Antiquities of the Jews*, I, 114, 115 (IV, 2, 3) : « *[Nimrod] gradually changed the government into tyranny, seeing no other way of turning men from the fear of God, but to bring them into a constant dependence on his power. He also said he would be revenged on God, if he should have a mind to drown the world again; for that he would build a tower too high for the waters to be able to reach! and that he would avenge himself on God for destroying their forefathers. Now the multitude were very ready to follow the determination of Nimrod, and to esteem it a piece of cowardice to submit to God; and they built a tower [...]; it grew very high, sooner than any one could expect* ». — See also Hugh Nibley's analysis on this topic in his study *The world of the Jaredites*, chapter 1.

[117] *Patriarchal Blessings*, Institute of Religion, January 17, 1964, p8.

[118] Josephus, *Antiquities of the Jews* Book I, chapter VI 2

[119] *The Holy Bible (KJV)*, Genesis 17: 20-21.

[120] *The Holy Bible (KJV)*, Genesis 36: 1-3.

[121] Darius Gray, *Blacks in the Bible*. www.fairmormon.org

[122] http://www.jewishencyclopedia.com/topic Jethro

[123] http://www.jewishhistory.org/hyksos-or-hebrews/ and http://jwa.org/encyclopedia/article/asenath-midrash-and-aggadah/

[124] R. K. Phillips, *The truth about Rahab*.

[125] http://jwa.org/encyclopedia/article/shuas-daughter-midrash-and-aggadah/

[126] *The Holy Bible (KJV)*, 1 Timothy 1 : 9

[127] St Ambrose, *Exposition of the Gospel according to St.Luke*, III 23-28: « *We must undoubtedly ascribe to a similar motive the fact that Ruth was not omitted, she whom the holy Apostle must have had in mind when he foresaw that the foreign peoples would be called to salvation through the Gospel : « The law is not made for a righteous man, but for the lawless and disobedient, for the ungodly and for sinners» (I Tim., I, 9). For how is it that Ruth, who was a foreigner, married a Jew? And why did the Evangelist feel that he had to mention, in Christ's genealogy, this marriage which was forbidden by the law (Deut., VII, 3)? The Lord then would not be descended from a legitimate marriage? This seems to be a disgrace: unless understood in the light of the Apostle's statement that « the law is not made for a righteous man, but for the lawless and disobedient, for the ungodly and for sinners» ». For Ruth was a foreigner and a Moabite. Besides, the Mosaic law prohibited such marriages, and excluded the Moabites from the flock — for it is written: «A Moabite shall not enter into the congregation of the Lord even to his tenth generation. » (Deut., XXIII, 3) — how then did she enter into the congregation, other than, because she was saintly and her behavior was beyond reproach, she was placed above the law? If, in fact, the Law is made for the ungodly and the sinners, it is certain that Ruth, who escaped the limitations of the Law, who entered into the congregation and became Israelite, who deserved being numbered among the ancestors of the Lord's race, chosen because of kindship of the soul and not of the body, is a great example to us: for in her is prefigured our entering into the Lord's congregation, we who are gathered from the nations* ».

[128] Newell G. Bringhurst, *The 'Missouri Thesis' Revisisted: Early Mormonism, Slavery, and the Status of Black People.*

Newell G. Bringhurst and Darron T. Smith (eds.) (2006). Black and Mormon (Urbana: University of Illinois Press) pp. 13–33 et p. 30.

[129] *The Holy Bible (KJV)*, Matthew 10: 5-6.

[130] *The Holy Bible (KJV)*, Matthew 15: 24.

[131] *The Holy Bible (KJV)*, Matthew 28: 19.

[132] *The Holy Bible (KJV)*, Galatians 3: 27-29.

[133] Brigham Young, *Journal of Discourses*, vol. 7, pages 290 - 291. Talk given during a conference in the Tabernacle on October 9th 1859.

[134] *The Holy Bible (KJV)*, Matthew 19: 30 and Mark 10: 31.

[135] *The Holy Bible (KJV)*, Luke 13: 30.

[136] *The Holy Bible (KJV)*, Matthew 15: 21-28.

[137] *The Holy Bible (KJV)*, Matthew 8: 5-11.

[138] *Pearl of Great Price*, Official Declaration n°2.

[139] Dallin H. Oaks, Interview with Associated Press, in Daily Herald, Provo, Utah, June 5th 1988.

[140] Scriptures guides – *Bless, blessed, blessing*

[141] *The Holy Bible (KJV)*, 1 Corinthians 12.

[142] *Doctrine and covenants* 130: 20-21.

[143] *The Holy Bible (KJV)*, Deuteronomy 11: 26-28.

[144] *Doctrine and Covenants* 89.

[145] *The Holy Bible (KJV)*, Joshua 1: 8.

[146] *The Holy Bible (KJV)*, Malachi 3: 10-11.

[147] *Millennial Star*, August 31th 1899, p. 547.

[148] *The Holy Bible (KJV)*, Malachi 3: 13-18.

[149] *Contributor* 6 : 297 ; quoted by Joseph Fielding Smith in *The Way to Perfection*, 1931, chapter 16, pp 98-99 in the French translation : « *Je crois que cette race est celle à laquelle furent consignés les esprits qui ne furent pas vaillants dans la grande révolte des cieux [...]*».

[150] *Wilford Woodruff's Journal*, entry of December 1869, also quoted by Joseph Fielding Smith in The Way to Perfection, 1931, chapter 16, pp 98-99 of the French translation.

[151] *Improvement Era*, April 1924, *The Negro and the Priesthood*.

[152] *Journal of Discourses*, Vol 1, pp 62-63, *Celestial Marriage*, Elder Orson Pratt, August 29th 1852.

[153] *Doctrines of the Gospel*, student manual, chapter 21: The foreordination of covenant Israel and their responsibilities.

[154] *The life and teachings of Jesus-Christ and His apostles,* chapter 30: God is no respecter of person.

[155] *The life and teachings of Jesus-Christ and His apostles,* chapter 41: Elected before the Foundations of the worlds.

[156] Harold B. Lee, *Understanding who we are brings self-respect*, General conference, October 5, 1973.

[157] Statement by the First Presidency under George Albert Smith, August 17th 1949.

[158] *Improvement Era,* April 1924, *The Negro and the Priesthood*.

[159] *Race and the Priesthood*, www.lds.org.

[160] *The Holy Bible (KJV)*, John 9: 2.

[161] *The Holy Bible (KJV)*, John 9: 3.

[162] *The Holy Bible (KJV)*, Job 8: 3 - 4.

[163] *The Holy Bible (KJV)*, Job 22: 4 - 10.

[164] *The Holy Bible (KJV)*, Job 1: 8.

[165] *The Book of Mormon*, Alma 34: 32.

[166] *Pearl of Great Price*, Abraham 3: 24-25.

[167] *The Holy Bible (KJV)*, James 1: 2 - 4.

[168] Ezra Taft Benson, *God's Hand in Our Nation's History in 1976 Devotional Speeches of the year*, 1977, p. 310.

Printed by
CreateSpace
4900 La Cross Road
North Charleston, SC 29406 USA

www.ingramcontent.com/pod-product-compliance
Lightning Source LLC
Chambersburg PA
CBHW060946040426
42445CB00011B/1016